All About Anime and Manga

The Art and Artists of Manga

Stuart A. Kallen

ReferencePoint Press

San Diego, CA

ReferencePoint Press®

About the Author

Stuart A. Kallen is the author of more than 350 nonfiction books for children and young adults. He has written on topics ranging from the theory of relativity to the art of electronic dance music. In addition, Kallen has written award-winning children's videos and television scripts. In his spare time he is a singer, songwriter, and guitarist in San Diego.

Printed in the United States

For more information, contact:
ReferencePoint Press, Inc.
PO Box 27779
San Diego, CA 92198
www.ReferencePointPress.com

Picture Credits:
Cover: Vuuji/Shutterstock
6: Ariana Ruiz/ZUMA Press/Newscom
10: Everett Collection
14: NBC/Photofest
20: Associated Press
23: Cartoon Network/Photofest
27: Kimimasa Mayama/Reuters/Newscom
31: Rat Pack Film Produktion GMBH/Constantin Film Produktion/Album/Newscom
33: Usa-Pyon/Shutterstock.com
37: Awana JF/Shutterstock.com
41: Dodotone/Shutterstock.com
43: Everett Collection/Alamy Stock Photo
46: ReferencePoint Press
50: Wachiwit/Shutterstock.com
54: Pictures from History/Bridgeman Images

LIBRARY OF CONGRESS CATALOGING-IN-PUBLICATION DATA

Names: Kallen, Stuart A., 1955- author.
Title: The art and artists of manga / by Stuart A. Kallen.
Description: San Diego, CA : ReferencePoint Press, 2022. | Series: All about anime and manga | Includes bibliographical references and index.
Identifiers: LCCN 2021030463 (print) | LCCN 2021030464 (ebook) | ISBN 9781678202200 (library binding) | ISBN 9781678202217 (ebook)
Subjects: LCSH: Comic books, strips, etc.--Japan--Juvenile literature. | Cartoonists--Japan--Biography. | Animated television programs--Japan--Juvenile literature. | Animated films--Japan--Juvenile literature.
Classification: LCC PN6790.J3 K35 2022 (print) | LCC PN6790.J3 (ebook) | DDC 741.5/952 [B]--dc23
LC record available at https://lccn.loc.gov/2021030463
LC ebook record available at https://lccn.loc.gov/2021030464

Contents

Introduction

Mangaka Make Art

In 2019 the Anime Expo attracted over 115,000 people from all over the world to the Los Angeles Convention Center. The expo, which is the largest anime convention in North America, would not exist without Japanese comics called manga. Almost all of the Japanese animated cartoons shown at the festival originated on the pages of manga. And the Anime Expo featured dozens of manga artists, called *mangaka*, who gave lectures, participated in panel discussions, and hosted artistic workshops. Some of the mangaka superstars included Bisco Hatori, known for the series *Ouran High School Host Club*, and Katsuhiro Otomo, creator of the manga and anime franchise *Akira*.

When the Anime Expo held its first convention in 1992, only around 1,750 dedicated fans of Japanese cartoons were in attendance. While manga was extremely popular in Japan at the time, the Japanese-style comics were just beginning to catch on in the

United States. Enjoying manga was a challenge for US readers raised on full-color American comics that had thirty-two pages. Most manga were printed in black and white then, as they still are today. Panel sequences unfold "backward" on the page from right to left. And some manga are as thick as books, with more than 350 pages.

There are also artistic differences between American comics and Japanese manga. In the United States, characters and scenes tend to be drawn in a realistic manner, whereas Japanese characters have exaggerated features. When manga characters cry, their tears pour out in torrents. When they laugh, their tiny mouths grow to engulf their faces while their huge eyes become tiny. An angry character will have steam coming from his or her entire body.

The Appeal of Whimsical Art

Humorous sketches were first called *manga* in Japan around two hundred years ago. The term, commonly interpreted to mean "whimsical pictures," was coined by renowned Japanese artist Katsushika Hokusai in 1814, but the word has a deeper meaning. The written Japanese symbol for the word *manga* denotes rough, rapid, spontaneous sketches made by an artist. The drawings are seen as improvised, done on a tide of artistic inspiration with no sense of order. This technique, which remains central to the manga style, provides a sense of page-turning excitement that gives Japanese comics their universal appeal.

While appealing to the masses, most mangaka work alone. They write the scripts for the stories and draw every panel themselves. Because manga are a black-and-white medium, most mangaka shun computers and digital art programs. Instead, they create art the old-fashioned way, with ink pens that allow them to draw sweeping dramatic lines that can range from light to very heavy. Mangaka also rely on what is called IC Manga Screen Tone. These are preprinted sheets with patterns, lines, and various tones that are used to give textures and shades to drawings. Screen Tone has adhesive backing, which allows the artist to apply it to the art and rub it on with a stylus. Screen tone lets mangaka work fast; some create dozens of pages of artwork every week.

Many mangaka dedicate their entire lives to their art. While some in Japan are revered like sports heroes and movie stars, it is customary for mangaka to keep a low profile. This leads some popular mangaka to avoid interviewers, photographers, and even their most dedicated fans. However, this has become more difficult as the popularity of manga has soared. In Japan the endless parade of demon slayers, gun-wielding pixies, magical supergirls, adorable ogres, frightening soul reapers, and talking cats generates more than $5.6 billion annually. And throughout the world, manga characters can be seen in video games, toys, live-action movies, costumes, jewelry, and more. Japanese literature professor Satoru Saito explains the widespread appeal of manga: "Many have children as protagonists. . . . [Stories] are told from

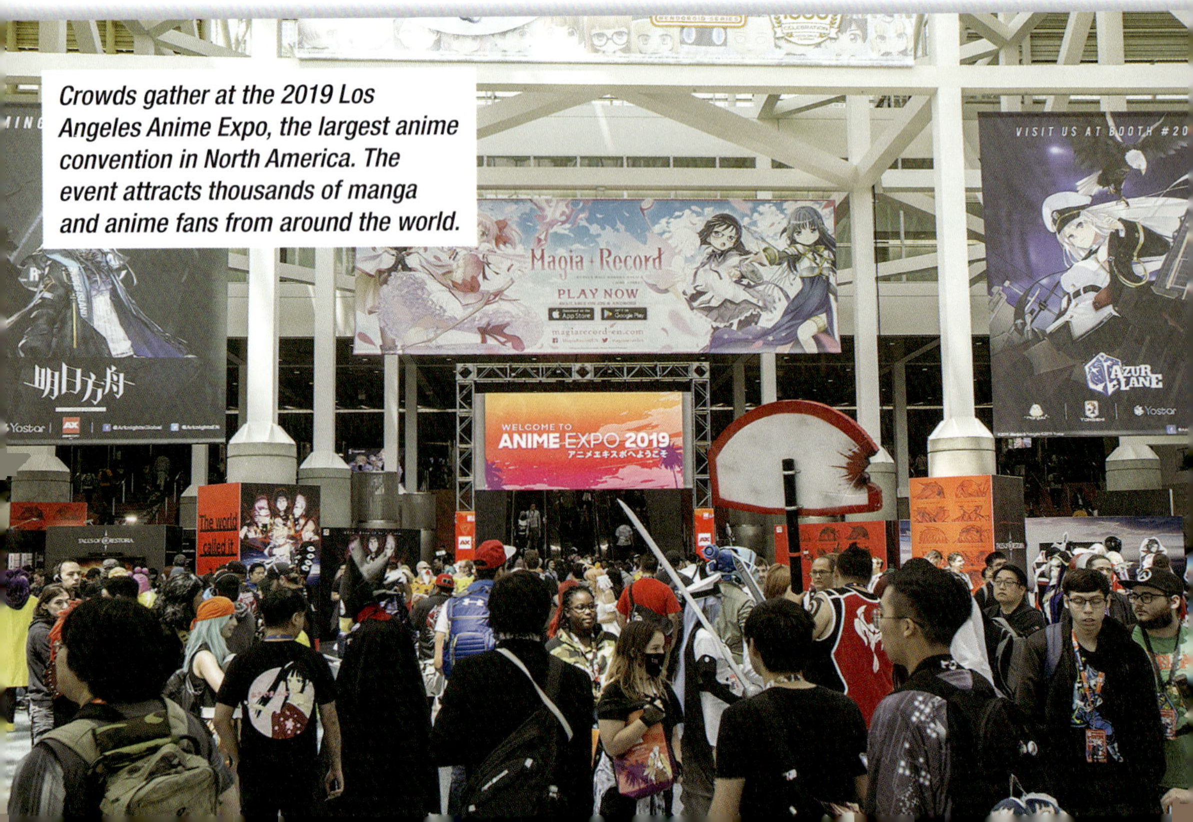

Crowds gather at the 2019 Los Angeles Anime Expo, the largest anime convention in North America. The event attracts thousands of manga and anime fans from around the world.

the perspective of children forced into the adult worlds of crime fighting or war, and illustrate the hypocrisies of the adult world through detailed descriptions of children's inner turmoil."[1]

"Comics are an international language, they can cross boundaries and generations. Comics are a bridge between all cultures."[2]

—Osamu Tezuka, manga pioneer

The mangaka focus on young heroes might explain why manga began outselling old-fashioned American superhero comics in the United States for the first time in 2019. Osamu Tezuka, who created Astro Boy and other popular characters, once explained the broad appeal of his work: "Comics are an international language, they can cross boundaries and generations. Comics are a bridge between all cultures."[2] Tezuka, who died in 1989, never lived to see his prophetic statement come true. But in the 2020s mangaka are spinning out creations in nearly every country on earth, including Iran, France, Brazil, Turkey, Indonesia, and the United States. And sales of manga grew 44 percent in 2020 over the previous year, according to NPD BookScan. With manga titles like *My Hero Academia* by Kohei Horikoshi and *One Piece* by Eiichiro Oda dominating the best-seller charts, the international language created by mangaka will continue to bridge cultures and cross boundaries for generations to come.

Chapter One

Osamu Tezuka

Osamu Tezuka was born in Osaka, Japan, in 1928. He was a brilliant child who loved to read and play piano, but his main inspiration came from the comic strips he saw in the newspaper. Some, like Pat Sullivan's *Felix the Cat*, originated in the United States, while others such as *Easy-Going Daddy* by Yutaka Asō were Japanese. Tezuka began copying the cartoons and inventing his own characters. He created his first comic strip at age nine.

While Tezuka's early comics were about happy children having fun, his peaceful middle-class existence was interrupted in 1940 when Japan entered World War II. Two million Japanese died during the war, and most of the nation's major cities were destroyed by American bombing raids. In August 1945 the war ended after the cities of Hiroshima and Nagasaki were incinerated by atom bombs. Like many Japanese, Tezuka personally witnessed the horrors of war; he saw hundreds of people in Osaka killed in what he later called a sea of fire—and the impact of this experience can be seen in many of his stories. After the war the United States occupied Japan until 1952.

Japan was extremely poor and in dire need of doctors to tend to the sick and wounded. Osamu's father was a doctor, and Osamu followed in his footsteps, earning a medical degree in 1946. All the while, however, he was still drawing comics. Before war's end he had created two thousand pages of drawings and had decided he wanted to become a comic book artist. There was zero demand for anyone with this skill.

Tezuka was fascinated by the cheap comic books called *akahon*, or red books, named for the bright red and orange ink used on covers to attract children who bought them in Japan's market stalls. Red books were printed on cheap paper by small publishers who hired young artists desperate for work. In 1947 Tezuka was one of those desperate artists, one who was willing to toil day and night to create a comic that would help launch his career. Working quickly, Tezuka produced 250 pages of drawings for a comic called *New Treasure Island*. The story followed a boy named Pete who finds a treasure map, sails off in pursuit of riches, and experiences a series of misfortunes. When it was published, Tezuka became an overnight sensation. *New Treasure Island* quickly sold over four hundred thousand copies.

A Revolution in Comics

New Treasure Island was unlike any other comic book. Loosely based on the 1883 pirate story *Treasure Island* by Scottish author Robert Louis Stevenson, *New Treasure Island* was unique in several ways. At the time, most Japanese comics were short and showed flat figures in square boxes. *New Treasure Island* weighed in at a book-length 190 pages. The drawings were cinematic, with panels that unfolded like scenes in a movie. Tezuka created scenes that zoomed in from a distance to extreme close-ups that might show only lines of emotion in a character's eyes and forehead. A series of wide panels that took in an entire landscape were reminiscent of a movie camera panning from side to side. Another technique showed the action from above, from below, and from unusual angles. These panels resembled quick cuts in

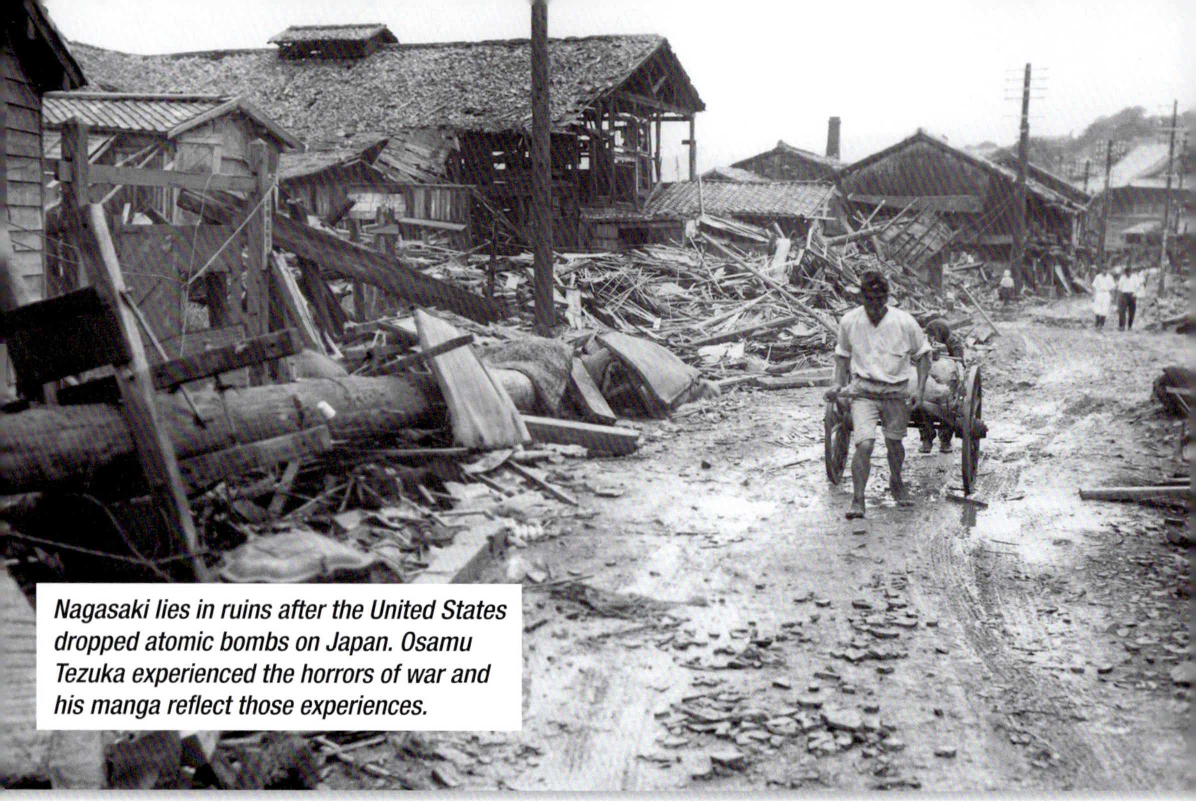

Nagasaki lies in ruins after the United States dropped atomic bombs on Japan. Osamu Tezuka experienced the horrors of war and his manga reflect those experiences.

a film that add tension and excitement. This style was inspired by the American innovator Walt Disney, whose comic books and award-winning animated films like *Snow White*, *Pinocchio*, and *Fantasia* were available in Japan before the war.

Tezuka deliberately broke with the past when he created *New Treasure Island*. He felt traditional comics, which were drawn as if an audience was viewing the action on a stage, were stale and boring. Shortly before his death in 1989, Tezuka described the innovative ideas and methods that made his work so appealing and noteworthy: "This [old style of drawing] made it impossible to create dramatic or psychological effects, so I began to use cinematic techniques. . . . I experimented with close-ups and different angles, and instead of using only one frame for an action scene or the

"I experimented with close-ups and different angles, and . . . I made a point of depicting a movement or facial expression with many frames, even many pages."[3]

—Osamu Tezuka, manga pioneer

climax (as was customary), I made a point of depicting a movement or facial expression with many frames, even many pages. The result was a super-long comic."[3]

New Treasure Island set sales records and revolutionized the comic book industry in Japan. According to manga reviewer Tadao Sato, "After Tezuka, it became not at all uncommon to see multi-volume comics with adventure-filled, sustained plots. . . . Tezuka's major achievement was widening the scope of comics, enabling them to achieve the same impact as novels, plays, or any other literary form."[4]

"Tezuka's major achievement was widening the scope of comics, enabling them to achieve the same impact as novels, plays, or any other literary form."[4]

—Tadao Sato, manga reviewer

While changing the publishing industry, Tezuka also inspired an entire generation of artists who sought to imitate his success. As the impact of *New Treasure Island* increased, another word was needed to describe Japanese comics and their creators. For reasons unknown, the word *manga*, first coined in the early nineteenth century, came into popular usage. Artists who created manga were called mangaka.

Showing Compassion

Tezuka's next project, serialized in three volumes from 1950 to 1954, was even more ambitious than *New Treasure Island*. The sprawling epic *Jungle Emperor* (known in the United States as *Kimba the White Lion*) follows a heroic white lion named Kimba who protects smaller jungle animals from brutal hunters. With *Jungle Emperor* Tezuka continued to experiment with visual storytelling. He reduced the need for written words by telling the story through character gestures and expressions and dramatic artistic compositions. (Some have noted that the Disney film *The Lion King* bears a strong resemblance to *Jungle Emperor*.)

Jungle Emperor was a hit, but Tezuka did not slow down. He worked long hours to create thousands of pages of new manga that failed to gain much public attention. These works included histories, detective stories, romances, and science fiction. Whatever the genre, Tezuka focused on several themes that grew out of the trauma of living through World War II and the American occupation of postwar Japan. His characters, like Kimba, often exhibited compassion for the weak and defenseless as they struggled heroically against the odds. And as Tezuka biographer Frederik L. Schodt explains, "[Tezuka's] revulsion for war [was] a theme that would permeate nearly all the works he later created. Moreover, he developed a lifelong interest in the complexity of human nature, a deep belief in the need to communicate with other cultures, and a belief in the power of manga and animation to help do so."[5]

Tezuka's most iconic character reflected his desire to communicate a message of peaceful coexistence to a wide audience. Tezuka created *Tetsuwan Atomu*, or *Mighty Atom*, in 1952. The character, a boy robot named Mighty Atom, was built by a mad scientist who was trying to replace his dead son. The *Mighty Atom* manga featured the newest technology under development in the 1950s, but the story was set in what was then the far distant future—April 7, 2003. Mighty Atom had a nuclear reactor heart, a computer brain, searchlight eyes, a machine gun in his backside, lasers in his hands, and rockets in his feet. The rockets propelled him through the air. He could understand sixty languages, had super hearing and vision, and could smash through concrete with his 100,000-horsepower strength.

Tezuka expertly used his pen strokes to show the Mighty Atom jumping off the page with power. He packed the panels of the manga with action words like *whoosh*, *smash*, and *voosh* written in elongated letters. Exciting scenes showed the Mighty Atom robot flying toward the reader or vanquishing evildoers with his powerful fists.

Despite his awesome powers, the Mighty Atom was also cute and cuddly. He was the size of a twelve-year-old boy, with giant expressive eyes, a button nose, and a sweet, child-

A Tribute to Osamu Tezuka

When Osamu Tezuka died in 1989, millions in Japan mourned his passing. Retrospectives of Tezuka's work appeared on television and in magazines. Politicians, celebrities, and average citizens offered somber eulogies to the mangaka who inspired so many people. Japan's most respected newspaper, *Asahi Shimbun*, ran an editorial called "Mighty Atom's Message," which urged young artists to pick up pens and create work that honored Tezuka's life. The paper also noted that Japanese people love comics more than people in any other nation. The editorial explained why that was the case:

> It is because in other countries they did not have Osamu Tezuka. The postwar comics and animation culture of Japan would never have happened without him. He was the creator of both story-based manga and television anime, and the influence of his attractive and androgynous boy character, Atom, with his long eyelashes, is easy to detect, not only in boys' manga, but also in the protagonists of the now oh-so-popular girls' manga.

Quoted in Frederik L. Schodt, *The Astro Boy Essays*. Berkeley, CA: Stone Bridge Press, 2007, p. vii.

like smile. And unlike American superheroes fighting for justice, Mighty Atom fought for equality and peace and mediated between warring factions.

Tezuka was still publishing his work in red books when he created *Mighty Atom*. But there was a growing interest in *shōnen* manga, literally "boys' comics," that were written primarily for males ages eight to eighteen. Tezuka initially created *Mighty Atom* at the suggestion of Takeshi Kanai, who edited the most popular monthly manga magazine, *Monthly Shōnen Magazine*. Kanai suggested giving the robot a human personality, saying, "Then the readers will identify with him, and think of him as a friend. . . . Make him a robot with emotions, who laughs, cries, and gets angry when he senses injustice!"[6]

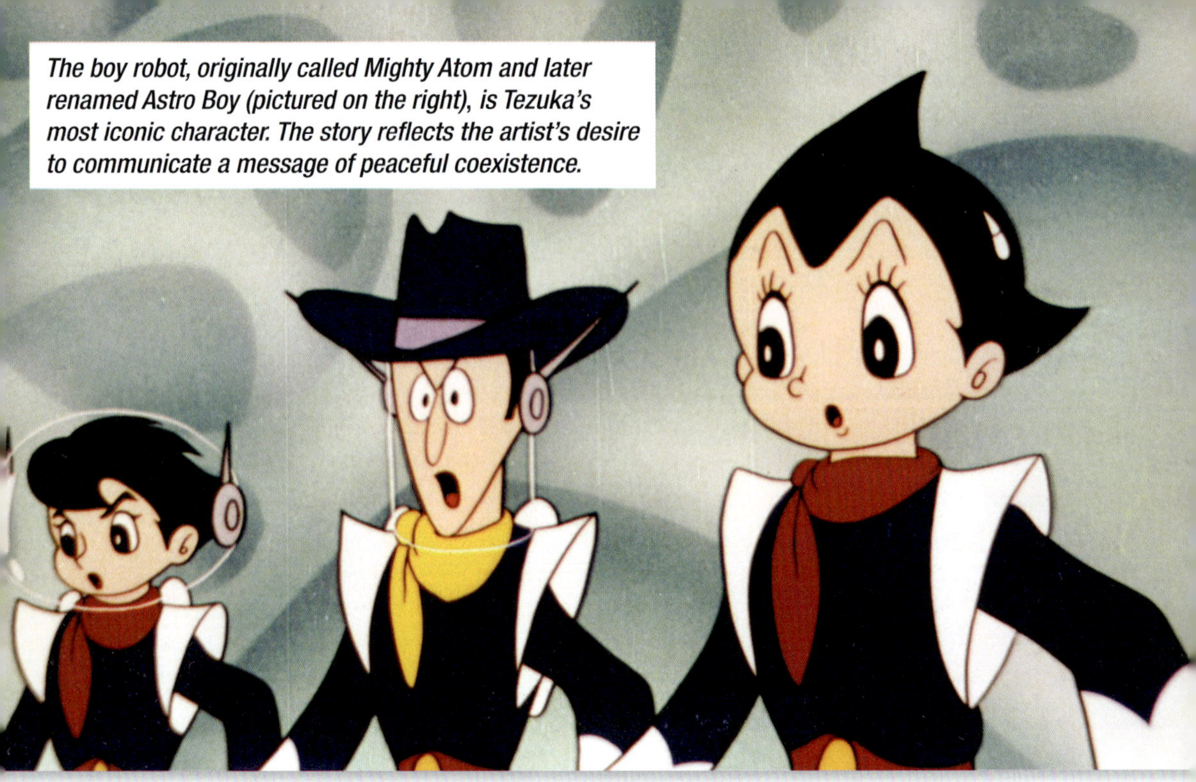

The boy robot, originally called Mighty Atom and later renamed Astro Boy (pictured on the right), is Tezuka's most iconic character. The story reflects the artist's desire to communicate a message of peaceful coexistence.

Kanai's suggestion, which aligned with Tezuka's basic philosophy, helped make *Mighty Atom* extremely popular. Tezuka began receiving hundreds of letters every day from Japanese schoolchildren who related to the boy robot. The character went on to appear in 112 episodes printed in 23 volumes of manga from 1952 to 1968. Reprinted countless times over the decades, *Mighty Atom* manga have sold over 100 million copies worldwide.

The First Anime

In 1963 Mighty Atom starred in Japan's first anime, or animated cartoon, which appeared on Fuji TV. The same year, the black-and-white cartoon was dubbed in English, renamed *Astro Boy*, and shown on the American NBC network on Sunday mornings. The cartoon was produced at the animation studio Tezuka founded in 1961. He called the studio Mushi Production, literally "Bug Production." Tezuka loved insects as a child, and a character based on a type of beetle called *osamushi* appeared in his earliest comics. This love of insects carried over to his later works. According to Schodt, there is a 290-page "field guide" published in Japan that features the various insects that appeared in *Mighty Atom* and other Tezuka manga.

The original *Astro Boy* was the first cartoon to introduce Japanese anime to American audiences. The low-budget animation could not rival the high-quality cartoons produced by Disney and others that were typically shown on Sunday morning TV. However, like children in Japan, American kids identified with the compassionate yet powerful robot. *Astro Boy* ran in the United States from 1963 to 1965. The show, which could be seen in reruns until the early 1970s in the United States, was also the first cartoon character to create a market for children's merchandise, which included Astro Boy action figures, puzzles, and other toys. *Astro Boy* appeared again in Japan in the 1980 anime *Shin Tetsuwan Atomu*. In 2009 the character was revived for the American 3-D anime film *Astro Boy*.

The Bird of Fire

While Astro Boy was a success, Mushi Production was not. Tezuka stepped down as director of the anime studio in 1968, and the company went bankrupt several years later. While Tezuka continued to experiment with anime for the rest of his life, drawing manga was his main focus after he left Mushi. But Tezuka wanted to move beyond shōnen manga. In 1967 he created a manga magazine called *Com* that featured experimental works by himself and others, including female mangaka.

Com published the first seven stories of the fantasy manga *Phoenix*, which Tezuka called his life's work. *Phoenix* consists of twelve volumes that jump back and forth in time from the year 270 CE to the year 3404 in the far-distant future. The stories are extremely complex, but most involve characters searching for immortality found in the blood of the phoenix, or bird of fire. The stories and artwork of *Phoenix* examined the meaning of life and death and pushed the artistic boundaries of manga. As reviewer Kris Kosaka writes:

> Artistically experimental, Tezuka's images sparked modern stylistic revolutions in visual design. He plays with framing and perspective as the narratives intensely engage with human concerns: betrayal, love, compassion, ambition. The epic scope of this series will amaze readers on several levels, drawing critical comparisons to everything from Shakespearean tragedy to early Walt Disney.[7]

Tezuka never finished *Phoenix*. He died of stomach cancer at age sixty in 1989. At the time of his death, few Americans had heard of the revered mangaka. However, in Japan Tezuka was lauded as *manga no kami*, literally the "god of comics." And his beloved boy robot was a national icon. On April 7, 2003, the Japanese celebrated the character's birthday as imagined by Tezuka when he created the character more than fifty years earlier. Eighty major corporations celebrated the event with toys, books, comics, music, and an array of merchandise, which generated over $5 billion.

"Artistically experimental, Tezuka's images sparked modern stylistic revolutions in visual design."[7]

—Kris Kosaka, reviewer

Tezuka's brilliance can be seen in *The Complete Manga Works of Tezuka Osamu*, published in Japan (where it is customary for surnames to precede given names). The work comprises eighty thousand pages of drawings in four hundred volumes. While impressive, those volumes contain a little over half of the artist's work. The god of comics is also honored in the Osamu Tezuka Manga Museum, founded in 1994 in the small town of Takarazuka, near Tezuka's birthplace.

Tezuka's influence remains alive far beyond the museum walls. Born in the ashes of a devastating war, he changed the face of

An Anime Pioneer

When Osamu Tezuka created the first Japanese anime, *Mighty Atom*, he was required by Fuji TV to produce the animation as cheaply as possible. This led Tezuka to invent production techniques that became industry standards in the 1960s. During this era, animation was produced with individual drawings made on transparent sheets of film called cels. Artists created the illusion of movement by drawing an image on a cel. Another cel was laid on top of the original, and the arms, legs, mouth, or eyes of the character would be moved very slightly. As more cels were layered onto one another, the character appeared to speak, blink its eyes, and make other movements. Companies like Disney created twelve different cels for every one second of movie film.

To cut costs, Tezuka's company created anime with only eight drawings per second of film. This resulted in jerky character movements. To cut production costs further, the characters in *Mighty Atom* sometimes spoke with their backs to the camera so no animation was necessary. While the jerky motion and lack of sophistication is a result of cost-cutting, it gives the anime a unique charm and style some say is missing from high-tech computer animation.

manga. His thrilling drawings portrayed the action of characters in such a way that has been described as a hybrid of manga and anime. And when compared to regular comics of the day, his long, cinematic stories made readers almost feel as if they were watching a film.

The modern manga industry owes its success to Tezuka, who provided entertainment, social commentary, and joy to countless fans. Tezuka described the reasons for his success shortly before his death: "[I] believed that comics were capable of more than just making people laugh. So in my themes, I incorporated tears, grief, anger, and hate, and I created stories where the ending was not always happy."[8]

Chapter Two

Naoko Takeuchi

In the late 1960s most young Japanese girls were given *shōjo* manga, or girls' comics, as soon as they could read. But the manga industry was dominated by men, who created unoriginal romance stories that featured lonely tomboys or unloved waifs. The tales usually ended with the main character marrying the boy of their dreams. But as competition in the manga industry increased, publishers were eager to print stories that would attract loyal female audiences ages eight to eighteen. This prompted publications like *Shōjo Comic* and *Nakayoshi* (*Best Friend*) to hire female mangaka. The switch to women artists increased shōjo manga sales, and by the early 1970s dozens of female mangaka had become famous for creating girls' comics. Coincidentally, many of the new artists were around twenty-four years old. Newspaper articles about the rise of female mangaka referred to the new generation of women artists as the *Showa 24* (Year 24) Group or the Magnificent 24s. The Magnificent 24s includes a group of venerated Japanese artists such as Yumiko Oshima, Riyoko Ikeda, and Moto Hagio.

While male mangaka working in the shōjo manga genre created formulaic romance stories, the Magnificent 24 artists broke barriers. They incorporated nontraditional notions of gender and sexuality and transformed traditional boys' genres like science fiction, horror, and historical fiction to include themes of interest to teenage girls. This meant creating stories that developed at a slower pace and focused on relationships, moods, daydreams, and longings.

> **"Time and reality were no longer always locked up inside [ruled borders outlining panels] and narratives could shift in and out of memories and dreams."[9]**
>
> —Paul Gravett, comic publisher

The Magnificent 24 also developed unique artistic styles that were more appealing to female readers. While male artists tended to draw rectangular, linear panels, the women dispensed with these uniform rows. Panels of differing shapes and sizes were used to highlight drama or action. As comic publisher Paul Gravett explains:

> The generation of female mangaka . . . softened the ruled borders outlining their panels, sometimes breaking them up, dissolving them or removing them all together. They overlapped or merged sequences of panels into collages. A borderless panel could now permeate the page, often beneath flotillas of other panels sailing across it. . . . Thus time and reality were no longer always locked up inside boxes and narratives could shift in and out of memories and dreams.[9]

Female mangaka incorporated other stylistic elements that made their work noteworthy. For example, female characters were drawn with huge, round, doll-like eyes and extremely long eyelashes. The enormous eyes of a shōjo character could take up half of the character's extremely large head, which itself might fill the entire page. This drawing style showed subtle expressions that demonstrated a character's inner thoughts, intimate feelings, and psychological makeup.

A Fan of Female Artists

Naoko Takeuchi, born in Kofu, Japan, in 1967, was one of those young fans who eagerly paged through the manga created by the Magnificent 24s. Takeuchi grew up reading shōjo manga like *Banana Bread Pudding* by Oshima and *They Were Eleven* by Hagio. And by the time Takeuchi attended high school in the early 1980s, she was drawing her own comics. Takeuchi joined both the manga and astronomy clubs at her high school, and—like all schoolgirls in Japan—she wore a sailor-style school uniform. These experiences would later play a large role in the creation of *Sailor Moon*, one of the first mangaka to endow young female characters with magical powers.

Takeuchi hoped to become a mangaka; her parents encouraged her to learn a profession in case her dream failed to come true. Takeuchi attended Kyoritsu University of Pharmacy and received a degree in chemistry at age nineteen. While working as a licensed pharmacist, Takeuchi created her first manga *Love Call*,

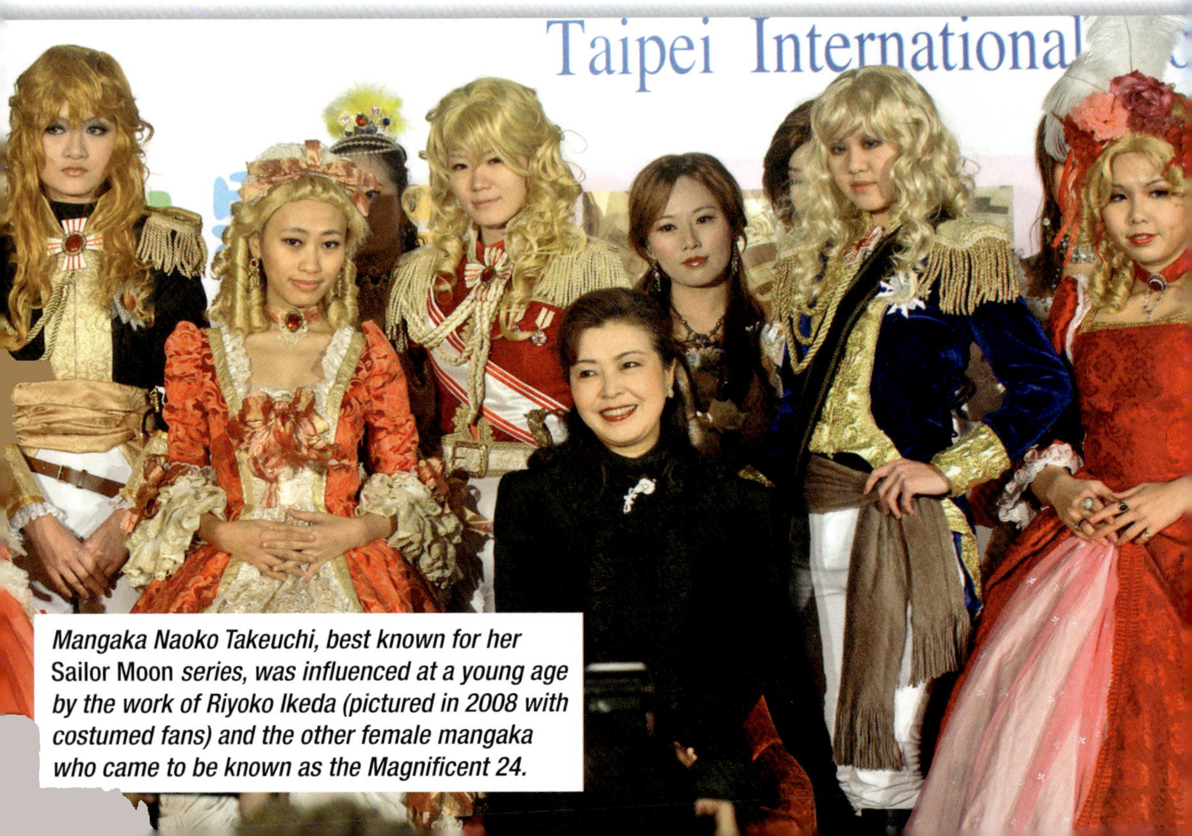

Mangaka Naoko Takeuchi, best known for her Sailor Moon *series, was influenced at a young age by the work of Riyoko Ikeda (pictured in 2008 with costumed fans) and the other female mangaka who came to be known as the Magnificent 24.*

The Founding Mother of Shōjo Manga

Moto Hagio, born in 1949, is one of the Magnificent 24s, a group of innovative female mangaka who rose to prominence in the 1970s. Hagio was known for her striking, often bizarre, imagery created with razor-thin lines and finely detailed facial expressions.

Hagio was never afraid to address topics that male mangaka long avoided. *The November Gymnasium* (1971) and *The Heart of Thomas* (1974) both focused on gay romance at male boarding schools. During this era homosexuality was considered taboo in Japanese society and was previously unmentionable in the world of manga. With these extremely popular works, Hagio is credited with inventing the manga subgenre known as *shōnen-ai*, or "boy love." These manga were girls' comics about romance between young men.

Hagio touched on other taboo subjects in her award-winning science fiction manga such as *They Were Eleven* and *The Poe Clan*. These stories covered fraught topics such as sexual abuse, childhood trauma, and aloof parents. By experimenting with style and content, Hagio redefined shōjo manga while fueling its explosive growth in the 1970s. These accomplishments earned her the title of founding mother of shōjo manga.

about a girl who falls in love with a disc jockey (DJ) at a music club. *Love Call* was published by Kodansha, a major manga publisher in Tokyo. In 1986 the work won the Nakayoshi Shinjin Manga Award for best newcomer. Takeuchi worked at Keio University Hospital while submitting one-shot, or single, manga stories to publishers. In a rare 1996 interview, Takeuchi recalled this period of her life: "I started drawing manga relatively late. I was a regular college student and got a regular job and then started drawing. So I have quite a few normal student and OL [office lady] friends."[10]

Takeuchi's next manga was a series called *Maria*, loosely based on the 1912 Jean Webster novel *Daddy-Long-Legs*. The manga story, written by the renowned novelist Marie Koizumi, follows a poor girl who is awarded a scholarship to a fancy private school, paid for by a mysterious anonymous man referred to as Daddy Long Legs. Maria's only requirement is that she write a letter to Daddy Long Legs each week describing her progress in school. Maria develops a crush on a boy whom she writes about in the letters.

The panels of *Maria* show Takeuchi's developing artistic style. The protagonist, Maria, is drawn with light sketchy lines that gives her an angelic, dreamy quality. Maria has large, expressive eyes, while her mouth and nose consist of nothing more than a few wispy strokes of the pen. Buildings and other characters feature heavier lines and solid blacks that contrast with Maria's airy features. Takeuchi's generous use of screen tone adds texture and shading to backgrounds and clothing.

Talking Cats and Magical Girls

In 1990 Takeuchi created *The Cherry Project*, about a girl named Asuka Chieri who was working to become a world-class figure skater. While working on *The Cherry Project*, Takeuchi decided she wanted to create a manga about crime fighters in outer space. Takeuchi says her editor had his own ideas: "I told my editor, 'I've always wanted to do a hero of justice story.' He told me in return, 'I'd like a heroine of justice in sailor suit.'"[11] In 1991 the ideas came together in the manga *Codename: Sailor V*. The story follows a thirteen-year-old middle school student, Minako Aino, who dreams about finding true love. However, Aino's life changes dramatically when she meets a talking cat that tells her she has powers to transform into a superwoman named Sailor Venus, or Sailor V. In the guise of Sailor V, Aino fights evildoers who are part of the Dark Agency.

Codename: Sailor V was immensely popular, and the Tōei Animation studio wanted to turn the manga into an anime. This inspired Takeuchi to create the series *Pretty Soldier Sailor Moon*, or simply *Sailor Moon*. The series follows a schoolgirl named Usagi Tsukino, who transforms into a girl with magical powers called Sailor Moon. She assembles a team, the Sailor Guardians, who

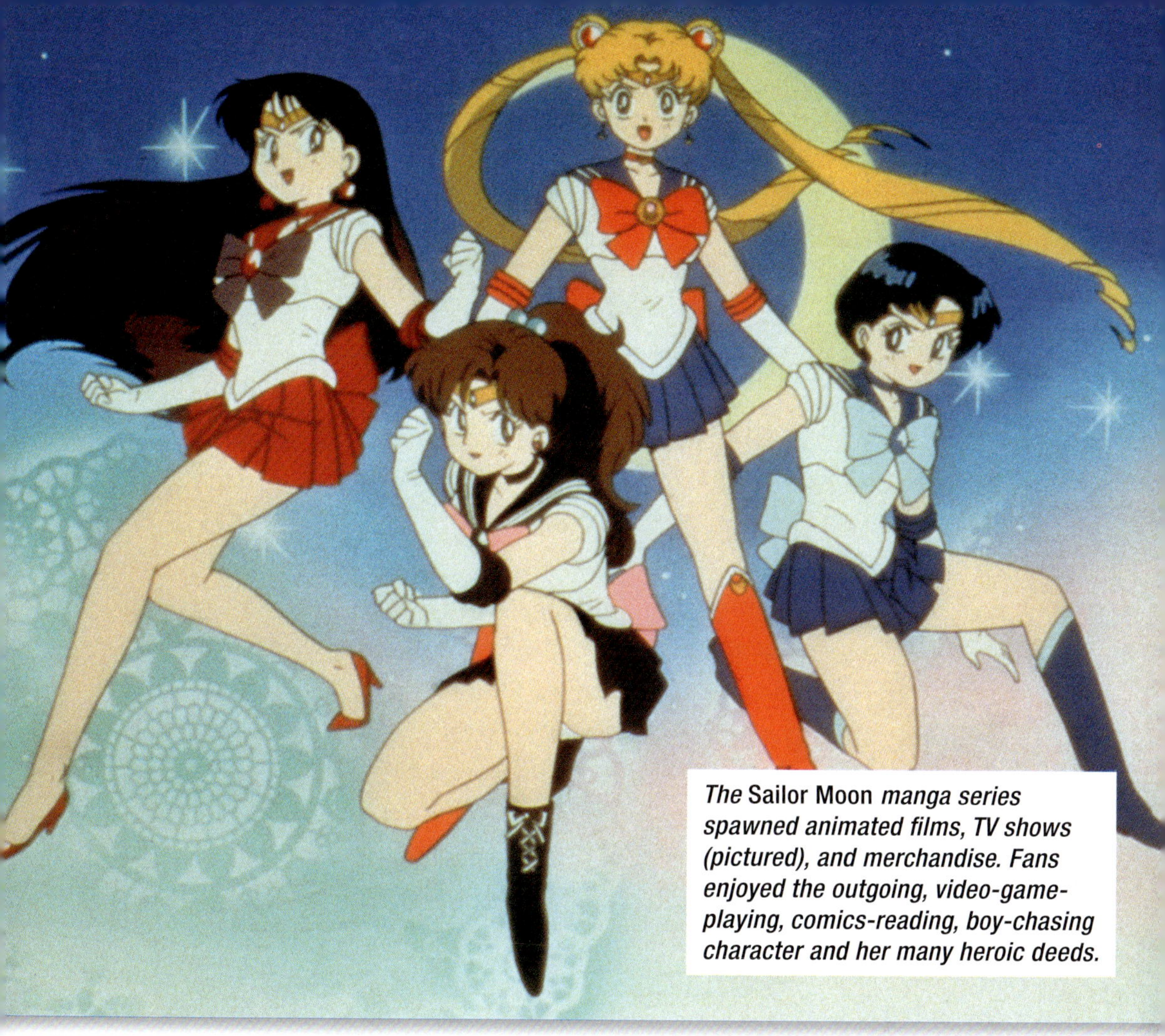

The Sailor Moon *manga series spawned animated films, TV shows (pictured), and merchandise. Fans enjoyed the outgoing, video-game-playing, comics-reading, boy-chasing character and her many heroic deeds.*

can transform from normal schoolgirls into crime-fighting heroes with supernatural powers. Sailor Moon, Sailor Venus, Sailor Mercury, Sailor Jupiter, and the others work to save humanity from evil. The Sailor Guardians battle dark forces from outer space, monsters from another dimension, and wicked life-forms bent on destroying the universe.

Sailor Moon was first published in *Best Friend* in December 1991. However, Takeuchi had to struggle with her publisher to get the manga into print. The men who ran *Best Friend* resisted creating a story featuring a squadron of five beautiful fighting girls. Traditionally, manga squadrons were nearly always male and consisted of a conventional cast of characters; one is a nerd with glasses, another is obese, one is strong but dumb, and so on. Takeuchi stood her ground:

> I thought, I'm going to show these old grandpas that beautiful girl characters can be good for business, and I'm not leaving my concept in the hands of old men. So I had to work hard to develop a sense of beauty and elegance in my characters, no matter what their type was. . . . The old man editors at "Nakayoshi" magazine thought I was being stubborn, and they didn't much care for the opinions of us lady authors, it was a difficult time.[12]

Takeuchi's instincts proved to be correct. Young girls instantly related to Sailor Moon and her Sailor Guardians, and *Best Friend* began outselling all other manga magazines.

Those who know Takeuchi say her personality resembles that of Usagi, who is an outgoing, video game–playing, comics-reading boy chaser. While Takeuchi laughs away such comparisons, she says she wanted her lead character's personality to contrast with her heroic deeds: "Heroes of justice tend to come from a specific type, but I wanted to make her unconventional. She's a crybaby and lazy and sometimes even cheats a little. I wanted to draw a normal girl like that. . . . Her selfishness and self-centeredness come to the surface too."[13]

"I'm going to show these old grandpas [running *Best Friends* manga] that beautiful girl characters can be good for business, and I'm not leaving my concept in the hands of old men."[12]

—Naoko Takeuchi, mangaka

Beyond the unique character profiles and story line, readers of *Sailor Moon* could spend hours simply enjoying Takeuchi's artwork. The facial features of the magical girls, the cute boys, and the evil monsters were far more detailed and expressive than characters seen in earlier manga. Planets,

The Eyes Tell the Story

In the 1970s female mangaka incorporated stylistic elements that made their drawings noteworthy. In the early 1980s male manga reviewers in Japan often criticized female mangaka for drawing characters with giant saucer-like eyes. Female mangaka responded by saying male reviewers misunderstood the function of eyes in shōjo manga. Japanese art and culture expert Mizuki Takahashi explains:

> What these critics overlooked was that the main purpose of shōjo manga was to show the complex inner psychology of the characters, not to create a realistic or action-filled tale. The aesthetic features, such as enormous eyes with long eyelashes, full-body portraits, and complicated panel designs are crucial for fans to engage emotionally with the story. . . . In regard to what these eyes signify, some have argued that starry eyes symbolize the love and dreams of the characters. . . . [They] also serve as mirrors that reflect the character's emotions. In other words, the eyes literally are the windows of the soul; by looking at the eyes, the readers can intuit the character's feelings, which remain unexpressed in dialog.

Quoted in Mark W. MacWilliams, ed., *Japanese Visual Culture*. Armonk, NY: East Gate Books, 2008, pp. 123–24.

stars, and skies explode with swirling tornadoes of action overlaid with written sound effects like *crackle*, *bang*, *shatter*, and *swoosh*.

A Best-Selling Hit

In 1994 Takeuchi won the Kodansha Manga Award. The sixty original chapters of *Sailor Moon*, serialized until 1997, made the manga one of the most popular of all time. Like other popular series, *Sailor Moon* was compiled in paperback books called *tankōbon* that contain multiple chapters of a single series. The eighteen volumes of *Sailor Moon* tankōbon have sold over 35 million copies in Japan.

The English-language version of *Sailor Moon* first appeared in the United States in 1997, and it quickly became the best-selling shōjo manga. The books were also exported to over twenty-three countries, including China, Mexico, Australia, the United Kingdom, and France. By the time *Sailor Moon* celebrated its twentieth anniversary in 2012, the manga had sold over 35 million copies in fifty countries. Journalist Aya Shounen explains why female readers related to Sailor Moon:

> An essential part of the story revolves around the bonds between women, and depictions of their friendships. Just hanging around, eating pizzas, talking all night long, or eating sweets and snacks. Of course, they face battles too, but in the end the main thing that brings them to victory is their cooperative effort. . . . Women everywhere are still desperately fighting society for their freedoms, and they have to have a tough skin to get by. I think that's why, universally, the sailor soldiers are such an inspiration.[14]

The *Sailor Moon* anime began airing in 1992 only a month after the first issue of the manga was published. While Tōei Animation only planned to produce the series for six months, the runaway success of the manga led the studio to create two hundred episodes, which aired for five years. Beginning in 1993, the *Sailor Moon* anime could be seen across Asia and Europe. In 1995 the *Sailor Moon* anime began airing in the United States. As the popularity of the manga and anime soared, *Sailor Moon* ignited a merchandise marketing bonanza. Over five thousand different items—including jewelry, clothing, video games, theme park attractions, companion books, novels, and toys—have been produced. The manga also generated three full-length anime films: *Sailor Moon R: The Movie* (1993), *Sailor Moon S: The Movie* (1994), and *Sailor Moon SuperS: The Movie* (1995). The TV series, *Pretty Guardian Sailor Moon*, was revived in 2003, while an animation adapted for the internet, called *Sailor Moon Crystal*, ran three seasons, from 2014 to 2015.

The *Sailor Moon* Empire

The success of *Sailor Moon* made Takeuchi an international celebrity. When a major earthquake struck Kobe, Japan, in 1995, she used her fame to raise money for victims. Takeuchi organized a benefit where she drew caricatures of guests, which were sold at auction. The drawings appeared as minor characters in *Sailor Moon* manga. In 1999 Takeuchi married the manga artist Yoshihiro Togashi, known for writing and illustrating the *Yu Yu Hakusho* and *Hunter x Hunter* manga series. The couple have two children. For relaxation, Takeuchi likes to drive her custom red Ferrari Spider.

With its long-running success, *Sailor Moon* occupied much of Takeuchi's time. She was involved in varying degrees in two live-action *Sailor Moon* movies, an ice-skating show based on the manga, and a theatrical musical with songs written by Takeuchi. During 1998 to 2004 Takeuchi created an autobiographical series

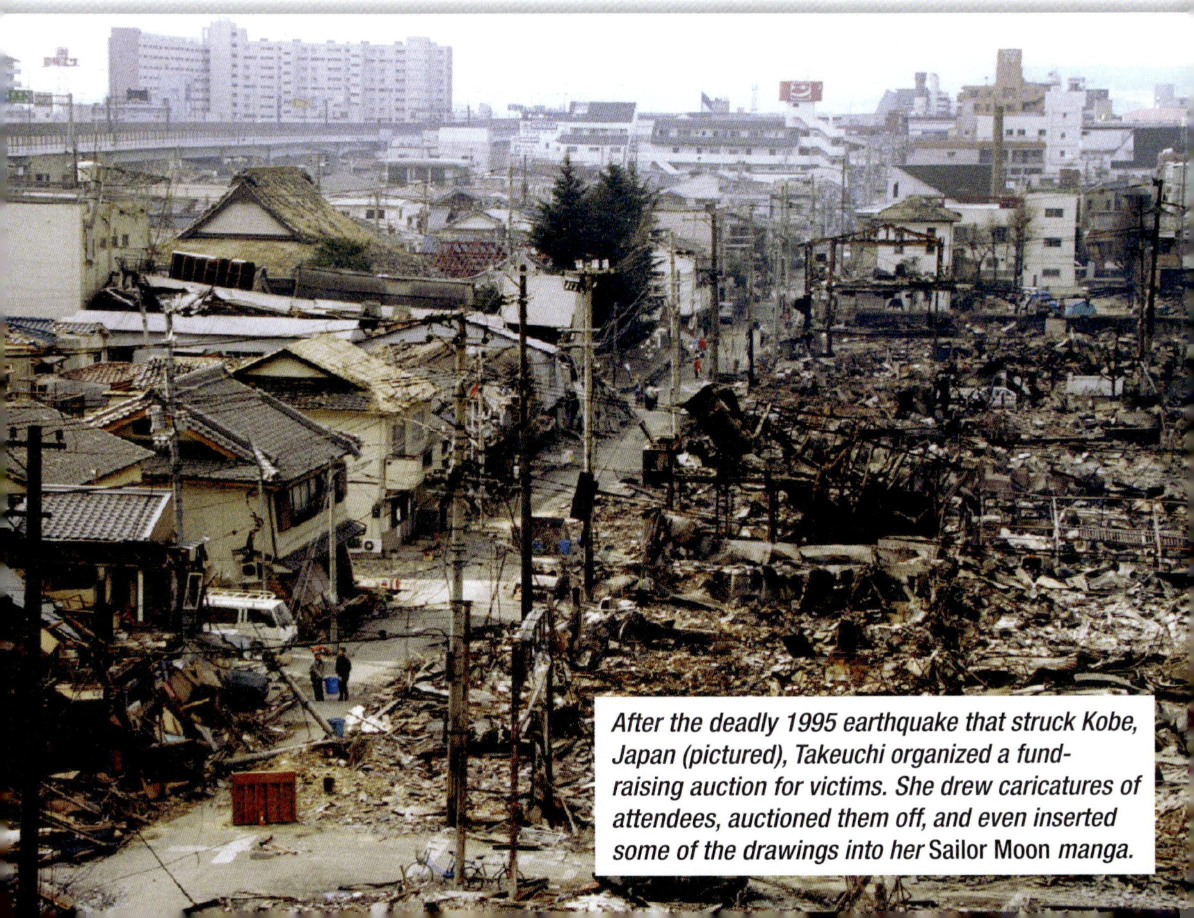

After the deadly 1995 earthquake that struck Kobe, Japan (pictured), Takeuchi organized a fund-raising auction for victims. She drew caricatures of attendees, auctioned them off, and even inserted some of the drawings into her Sailor Moon *manga.*

of comic strips called *Princess Naoko Takeuchi's Return-to-Society Punch!!!* These strips describe the mangaka's life after she finished working on *Sailor Moon*, including details about meeting her husband and starting a family.

Takeuchi's other manga have not been as successful as *Sailor Moon*. Her 2002 manga *Love Witch*, about a girl who finds a mysterious bottle of perfume that turns her into a witch, only ran for three chapters before it was discontinued. The series *Toki Meca*, about a robot and her creator, ran periodically from 2002 to 2006.

"[*Sailor Moon*] teaches girls to be proud of who they are, find power in their femininity, and make choices that build healthy relationships."[15]

—Jessica Lord, manga journalist

Apart from her other endeavors, *Sailor Moon* has become an economic engine that has generated at least $13 billion, according to the *Japan Times*. In 2021 Takeuchi was worth an estimated $52 million. Little wonder she says she is *Sailor Moon*'s biggest fan. But there are millions of others who love Sailor Moon and all she symbolizes. As manga journalist Jessica Lord writes, "[*Sailor Moon*] teaches girls to be proud of who they are, find power in their femininity, and make choices that build healthy relationships. All that coupled with action and romance makes *Sailor Moon* an amazing series that offers a lot to its target audience. And that's more than can be said for most media aimed at young girls."[15]

Chapter Three

Eiichiro Oda

Eiichiro Oda was twenty-two years old in 1997 when he launched the hugely popular *One Piece* manga series. The story follows the treasure-hunting adventures of the young pirate Monkey D. Luffy and his gang, the Straw Hat Pirates. Oda developed his love of seafaring pirates as a young boy watching the anime television series *Vicky the Viking*, based on a 1963 book by Swedish author Runer Jonsson. The show follows Vicky, a nine-year-old Viking boy who is weak and shy but very smart. He uses his brains to help his father and other villagers get out of dangerous situations.

While it might seem unlikely that eleventh-century Viking explorers would influence a best-selling manga, Oda was inspired by the series. He says, "As I did research on pirates for *One Piece*, I realized that Vikings are a type of pirate. I feel that it's awesome to have friends on your team, just like in the [*Vicky the Viking*] series. It may not be the best comparison, but I feel like that series' spirit is carried on within my work."[16]

From Wrestling to Westerns

While Oda was absorbing the spirit of *Vicky the Viking*, like most Japanese boys he was an early fan of shōnen manga. He loved the manga series *The Monster Kid* by the mangaka Fujiko A. Fujio and says he copied the panels endlessly. Oda claims that by 1979, when he was four years old, he had already decided to become a mangaka for one succinct reason: "Because you don't have to do a real job."[17] Oda's idea was reinforced in 1984 when the immensely successful manga series *Dragon Ball* appeared in *Weekly Shōnen Jump*. The action-packed series about a martial arts fighter, written and drawn by Akira Toriyama, had a profound influence on Oda. He began drawing his own manga characters, including a wresting panda called Pandaman. When Oda was twelve he submitted the drawing to the wrestling manga *Kinnikuman*. The editors liked Pandaman, and Oda's creation appeared as a minor character in one chapter. Oda kept the wrestling panda alive; Pandaman is sometimes seen mixed in with crowds of people in *One Piece*. There is also a female version of the character known as Pandawoman.

At age seventeen, Oda quit his high school soccer team so he could concentrate on drawing manga. He enjoyed westerns, which led him to create a one-shot cowboy manga with supernatural elements called *Wanted!* This manga, which Oda called a gag western, won second place in the respected Tezuka Awards in 1992. This helped Oda land a job as an assistant artist at *Weekly Shōnen Jump*. During his time at the magazine, Oda developed a reputation as a hard worker and a perfectionist. He worked side by side with some of the industry's leading mangaka, including Shinobu Kaitani, creator of *Midoriyama Police Gang*. Oda also spent eighteen months assisting the mangaka Masaya Tokuhiro with the production of *Mizu no Tomodachi*

"When I was in middle school, I decided that I would draw a pirate comic in [*Weekly Shōnen*] JUMP."[18]

—Eiichiro Oda, mangaka

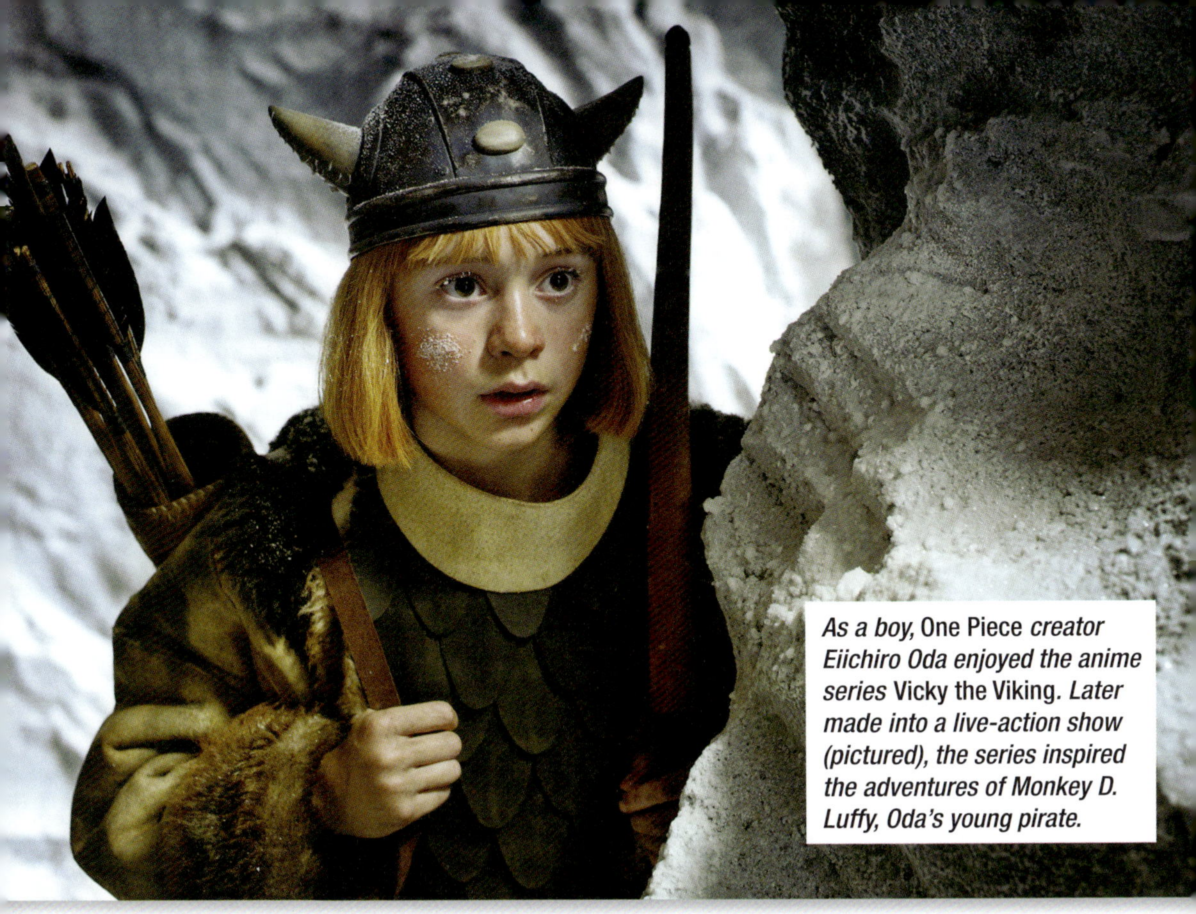

As a boy, One Piece *creator Eiichiro Oda enjoyed the anime series* Vicky the Viking*. Later made into a live-action show (pictured), the series inspired the adventures of Monkey D. Luffy, Oda's young pirate.*

Kappaman. During this period, Oda refined his techniques for drawing backgrounds and crowd scenes.

Oda began sketching out the characters for what would eventually become *One Piece* while working as an assistant at *Jump*. Initially, Oda created a manga called "Romance Dawn" that featured a pirate named Monkey D. Luffy. The story, which ran in *Jump* in 1996, was a one-shot that attracted hundreds of fan letters.

Monkey D. Luffy, with his signature straw hat, red vest, and sandals, went on to star as the main character in *One Piece*. When the first chapter of *One Piece* was published in July 1997, Oda added a short remark to *Jump*'s table of contents that dismissed the fact that pirates were murderous criminals and explained his fascination with the subject: "When I was in middle school, I decided that I would draw a pirate comic in JUMP. I'll ignore the atrocities of historic facts and just draw a bunch of jolly pirates. 'Cause hey, it's summer."[18]

The World of Monkey D. Luffy

Like his creator, Monkey D. Luffy was fascinated by pirates at an early age. At seventeen, Luffy recruited a crew and set sail to find a mythical treasure called One Piece that would allow him to become King of the Pirates. The One Piece treasure contains the wealth of the entire world, and every pirate is fighting to obtain it. But Luffy has an advantage. He accidentally eats the supernatural food called Devil Fruit, which gives his body the properties of rubber. This allows Luffy to stretch his limbs and his body to deliver kicks, punches, head butts, and other defensive maneuvers. While the Devil Fruit gives Luffy incredible strength, energy, and elasticity, it takes away his ability to swim, and his special powers disappear when he is submerged in water. This is a great disadvantage in the watery *One Piece* world that consists mostly of oceans.

Hundreds of other characters populate *One Piece*, including pirate gangs, giants, fish-men, animal creatures called minks, massive ship-destroying water creatures called sea kings, and fish-human hybrids called merfolk. They live in an ocean body called the Grand Line, which is ruled by the World Government. This corrupt organization destroys its enemies using secret agents, assassins, and powerful pirates known as the Seven Warlords of the Sea.

"We meet many characters, good and bad, incredibly well defined and, in most cases, with credible dreams and ambitions explaining the way they act."[19]

—Juan de Dios Dougnac, manga reviewer

The world that Oda created for Luffy's adventures is extremely complicated, even by manga standards. The story mixes humor, puns, and Luffy's innocent idealism with shocking real-world-type events that include bloody combat, slavery, government corruption, and mass murder. And as reviewer Juan de Dios Dougnac explains, Oda is a master when it comes to developing characters that feel alive and realistic: "As the plot goes on we

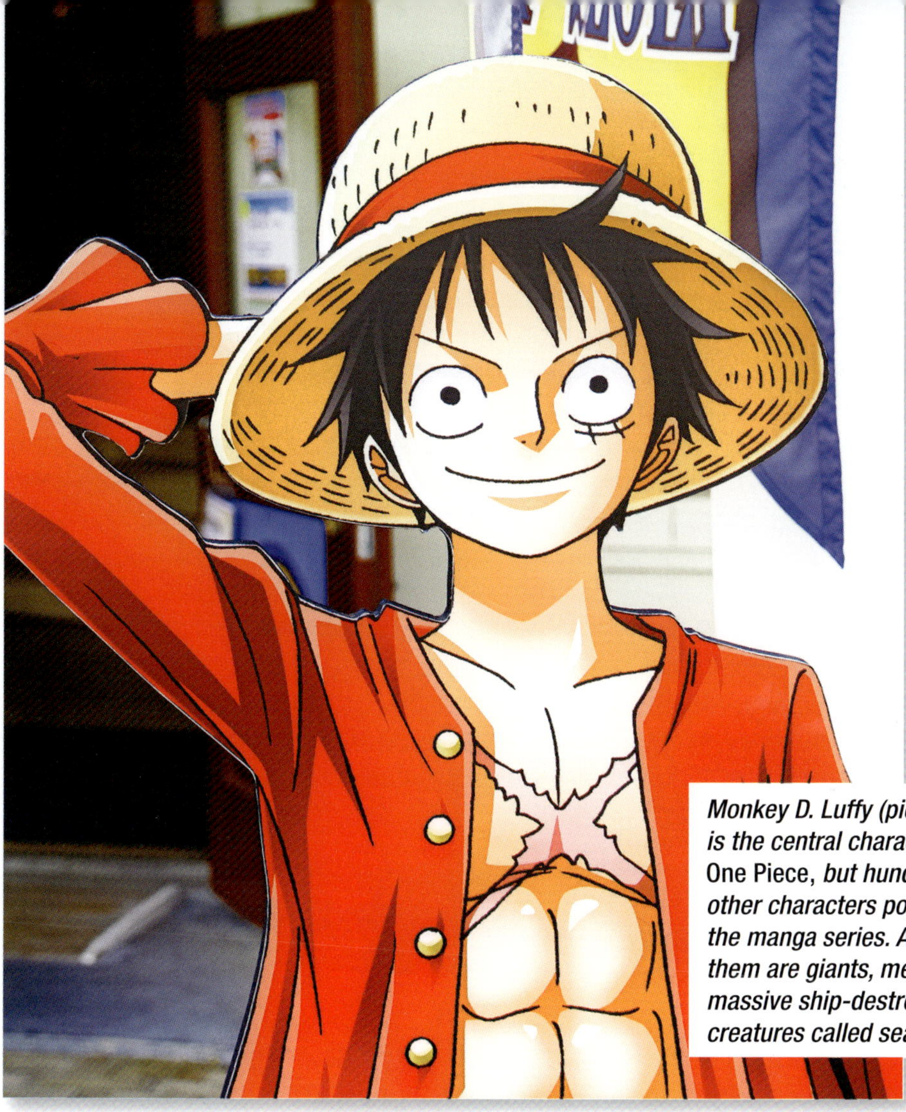

Monkey D. Luffy (pictured) is the central character of One Piece, *but hundreds of other characters populate the manga series. Among them are giants, merfolk, and massive ship-destroying water creatures called sea kings.*

meet many characters, good and bad, incredibly well defined and, in most cases, with credible dreams and ambitions explaining the way they act. From Luffy to secondary characters . . . they all have reasons to act like they do. Some reasons are good, others bad, but all of them are plausible."[19]

Awesome Artistic Abilities

Oda's storytelling abilities helped make *One Piece* successful, but the artistic style that he developed specifically for the series also helps set the manga apart. While some mangaka work to create scenes that are somewhat realistic, Oda's work is described as

Oda's Art Supplies

Eiichiro Oda has hand drawn over one thousand chapters of *One Piece* since he began sketching and inking the countless manga panels in 1997. Oda has also created an unusually large number of double-page color spreads. This is rare, since most mangaka do not have the time to color more than two pages of a chapter while maintaining their weekly production schedules.

Oda sometimes discusses the art tools he uses on *One Piece.* He creates his initial sketches with pencils; he prefers Mitsubishi 9800 art pencils. When inking the drawings, Oda prefers a Zebra Comic Pen Nib G Model. The nib is the metal part of the pen that is dipped into black ink. It attaches to a wood pencil-like nib holder. Many mangaka favor the Zebra Nib G, and it requires great skill to use properly. When Oda creates a color spread, he uses refillable Copic Sketch Markers. These professional-grade color markers are expensive—around $400 for a set of seventy-two colors. These markers allow artists to layer and blend colors seamlessly. And like all artists, Oda makes mistakes; he uses art gum erasers to remove pencil lines and white ink to make corrections on black images.

cartoonish. His characters have comically exaggerated features like long, pointy noses and bizarre unhinged jaws that drop to the ground when surprised.

Oda's style has matured over the years. In the first chapters of *One Piece*, he drew his characters in a bubbly cartoon style with thick lines and rounded features. As time passed, his lines grew thinner and his characters took on a sharper, more detailed appearance. And as the story grew in complexity, Oda began creating extremely crowded scenes filled with as many characters as he could pack into a single panel. Oda explained his artistic motivation in a 2012 interview: "Whenever I draw manga, I have only one reader in my mind—myself as a 15-year-old. I have no idea how other people would feel, so I turn back to the 15-year-old me to make a judgment on what is awesome or not.

I always try to stay true to myself, and somehow it resonates with the kids who read my manga."[20]

Oda's awesome artistic abilities can be seen in a video the *One Piece* staff posted to Instagram in June 2020. It shows Oda creating an action-packed color spread that was published in *Weekly Shōnen Jump*. The time-lapse scene features the character Sanji working as a DJ at a turntable. Oda makes rough sketches of the main characters, then comes back with his Zebra Nib G ink pen to finalize the drawing and create the backgrounds. The single panel features fifteen human and nonhuman characters cheering, dancing, and enjoying the music while the turntables, speakers, and other club features are drawn in fine detail. The scene is filled in with color markers to finalize a panel that could be viewed as both a cartoon and an artistic masterpiece. While the one-minute video is presented in fast motion, it takes Oda about thirty minutes to create a single color panel in this manner. (Oda uses up to five art assistants, who help him ink backgrounds, apply adhesive screen tone, and perform other tasks. They did not take part in the video production.)

"Whenever I draw manga, I have only one reader in my mind—myself as a 15-year-old."[20]

—Eiichiro Oda, mangaka

A Massive Success

One Piece was a massive success almost from the instant it was released in late 1997. Initially, Oda planned to end the series after five years, but *One Piece* took on a life of its own. As the story grew increasingly complex, Oda realized he could not tell it in that shortened time frame. Plus, he was having so much fun working on *One Piece* that he wanted to continue. As *One Piece* passed its nineteenth anniversary in 2016, an interviewer asked Oda how much of the story was completed. Oda replied, "I'd say about 65%. I need the courage to chip away at the ideas I come up with. It's a race against time between my remaining lifespan and the end of the series."[21] *One Piece* fans did not read much into such statements. Oda said the series was half done in 2006, a statement he repeated the following year.

Whatever the outcome of *One Piece*, Oda was undoubtedly driven to continue by the manga's record-breaking sales figures. *One Piece* sold over 100 million tankōbon volumes by 2005, and that number doubled to 200 million by 2011. This made *One Piece* the best-selling manga of all time. In 2015 the manga of Luffy's adventures entered the Guinness World Records for selling nearly 321 million copies. In 2021 *One Piece* surpassed the American superhero comic *Batman* in popularity, with total sales of over 484 million worldwide.

Oda has had little time to enjoy his success. On several occasions he has told interviewers that he sleeps only three hours a day, rising at 5:00 a.m. and working until 2:00 a.m., only pausing for meals. He spends the first half of the week sketching storyboards—rough drawings of scenes that can be pinned to a corkboard in chronological order. This allows Oda to move, add, or remove sketches to alter the look or layout of the pages. After the storyboards are laid out, Oda writes the manuscript for the chapter, then goes on to draw each panel. He says that the stories do not come easily to him; he creates the chapters by diligently sitting at his desk while making dozens of sketches that might never be used.

Oda maintains his grueling schedule by drinking a lot of coffee and caffeinated cola. When asked about this unhealthy lifestyle in 2016, Oda said:

> I work towards my deadlines, so I'm just as busy as when I was younger, and I've managed to pull it off each time with three hours of sleep. And if I do sleep more hours, I'll have to take those hours away from something else I have to do. I don't like that, so my hours haven't changed. If I decide that I'm going to sleep for four hours, it makes me

dread that I'll have to sleep an extra hour. But after turning in the manuscript, I give myself one day to get plenty of sleep.[22]

Some of the other things Oda was referring to include his family. In 2004 Oda married Chiaki Inaba, a model and actress. Inaba gave birth to a baby girl in 2006, and the couple had a second daughter in 2009. Because of his demanding work schedule, Oda does not live with his family. His wife and children visit him once a week.

The *One Piece* Kingdom

Oda's relentless commitment to *One Piece* has helped make it one of the most profitable media franchises of all time. The *One Piece* anime television series premiered in Japan in 1999 and has been in production ever since. By 2021 over 960 episodes of the series had been produced. The show has consistently rated among the top animated shows in Japan, and *One Piece* is

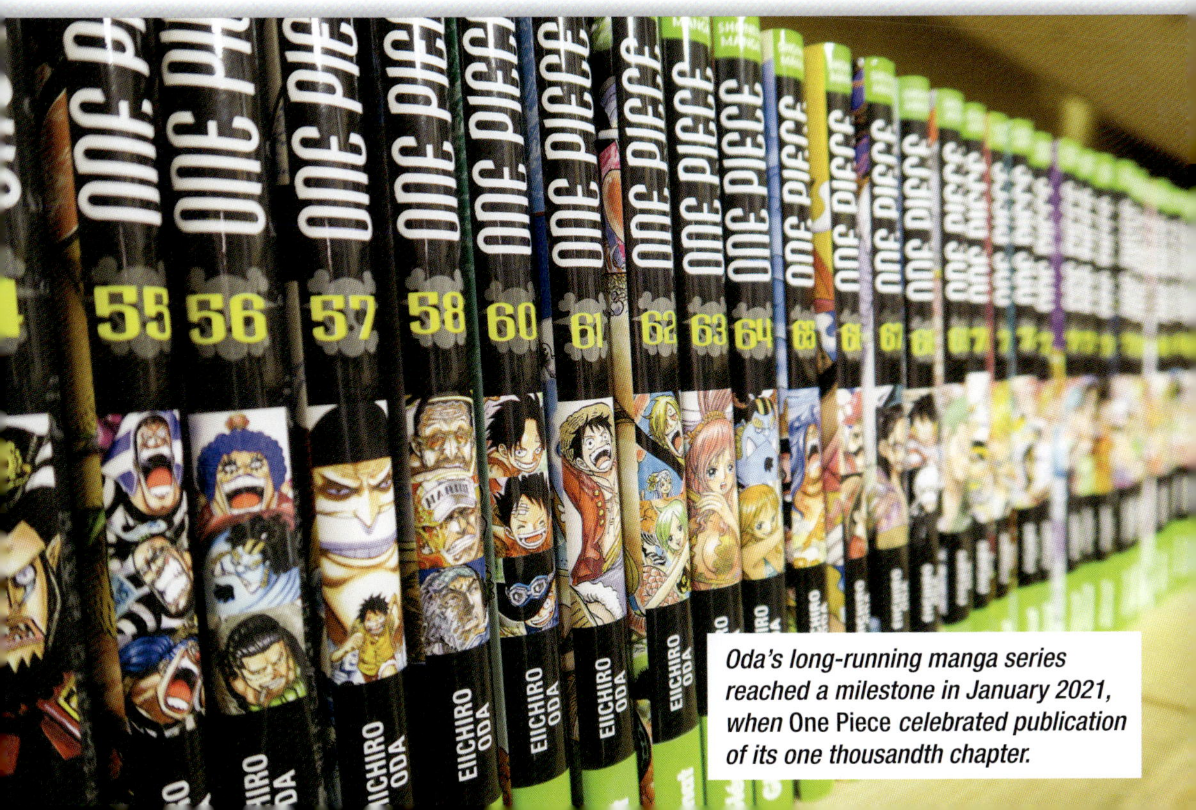

Oda's long-running manga series reached a milestone in January 2021, when One Piece *celebrated publication of its one thousandth chapter.*

also an international hit. Online episodes are sometimes viewed nearly 2 million times on streaming video platforms around the world. The story also generated a mind-boggling fourteen feature films during 2000 to 2019. Together these anime productions have made over $511 million as of 2021. Oda's net worth in 2020 was an estimated $200 million, according to finance website Money Inc.

One Piece has also generated an array of other items. These items include more than one hundred soundtrack CDs from films and the TV series, at least fifty-six video games based on the manga, ten novels, and nine related art books. When taken with

One Thousand Chapters

In January 2021 the one thousandth chapter of *One Piece* was published to much acclaim and celebration. Creator Eiichiro Oda marked the occasion with a letter to fans, excerpted below:

> **1000 Chapters!! I, uh, wow. . . . Words pretty much fail to describe the whirlwind these past 23 years have been. Literally half of my life has revolved around the almighty WEEKLY SERIALIZATION hehe. But it's not just me, Luffy and the Strawhats have navigated themselves to so many different islands and found themselves caught up in so many adventures. At this point, even I'm not sure how many lives they've touched along the way! . . . I convinced myself that I shouldn't get too full of myself because my readers would eventually leave the series and move on with their lives. Let me say that all of you have put me to shame for thinking such a thing. Your belief in Luffy has led me to believe in all of you, and that is what allows me to continue drawing exactly the kind of manga I want to draw. . . . My story is a long one. But for just a while longer, please watch over Luffy and his crew as they continue their adventure!**

Quoted in Joseph Luster, "One Piece 1000th Chapter Celebration Has the Series Going All Out," *Otaku USA Magazine*, January 3, 2021. https://otakuusamagazine.com.

the array of toys, clothing, and other *One Piece* items, Oda's pirate story has generated more than $5.5 billion, according to the merchandising company Bandai Namco Holdings.

The End Is in Sight

In January 2021 *One Piece* celebrated publication of its one thousandth chapter with a full-color ad in the *New York Times*. The ad asked readers to vote for their favorite character, and of course, Monkey D. Luffy was selected as number one. As part of the festivities, Oda released a statement encouraging fans to stay loyal: "So here we are, ready to dip our toes into the final stages of the story. It's taken us a long time to reach one thousand chapters. However, it's because I've completed a thousand chapters that you must believe I'll take us to the end. The story waiting for you will defy expectations! I mean it!!"[23]

There is little doubt that when *One Piece* ends, it will go out with a bang. And maybe Oda, who turned forty-six in 2021, will be able to start enjoying the life he imagined as a four-year-old. Either way, *One Piece* has become a permanent part of the manga universe and will continue to make readers turn pages in joy and excitement long after Oda puts down his pen and takes a break from his all-consuming dedication to Monkey D. Luffy and his crazy cast of characters.

Chapter Four

Hiromu Arakawa

The manga *Fullmetal Alchemist* follows the story of a twelve-year-old blond boy with a ponytail named Edward Elric and his younger, armor-plated brother, Alphonse. The Elric brothers practice alchemy as they travel through the war-torn land of Amestris, which vaguely resembles northern Europe in the early twentieth century. A casual reader of *Fullmetal Alchemist* might think that the manga's creator, Hiromu Arakawa, was a trained chemist. Her protagonists are empowered to rearrange the basic building blocks of matter on a molecular level through the use of alchemy. This allows them to fight off attackers by transforming the iron in blood into a razor-sharp sword while turning the mineral elements of stone into the bars of a prison. Evildoers in *Fullmetal Alchemist* use similar powers; they transmute fire, water, and other substances into deadly weapons.

While there are plenty of chemical reactions in *Fullmetal Alchemist*, Arakawa is no scientist. She is, however, a classically trained artist who took oil painting classes for seven years while working on her family's dairy farm in Makeubetsu, a rural village on the island of Hokkaido in northern Japan. Arakawa, born in 1973, began drawing at a young age—as soon as she could hold a pen. She had several dreams as a child: "I wanted to be a livestock farmer, but also taking care of animals in a zoo. And also becoming a mangaka. Growing up, this last one stayed. I explained it one day to my parents. I loved working [on] the farm, but I loved drawing above all."[24]

Her First Manga

The village where Arakawa lived did not have a bookshop that sold manga. However, a small rice market had a selection of books and magazines. Arakawa was around eight years old when she visited the shop to purchase her first manga. *Urusei Yatsura* is a romantic comedy in a science fiction setting created by Rumiko Takahashi, who is known as the Princess of Manga. The story of *Urusei Yatsura*, released from 1978 to 1987, unfolds after extraterrestrials invade Earth and dare humans to participate in a game of tag. If a human can touch the horns of the beautiful, bikini-clad alien named Lum Invader, humanity would not be enslaved.

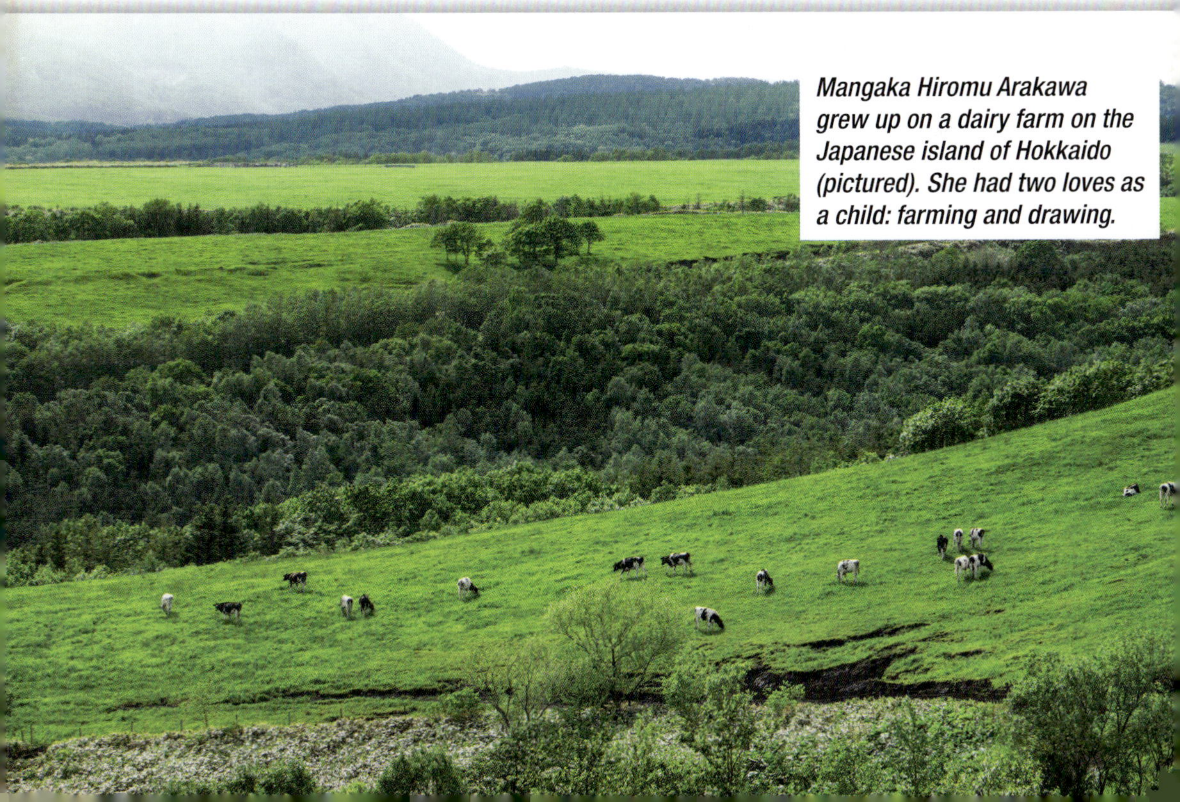

Mangaka Hiromu Arakawa grew up on a dairy farm on the Japanese island of Hokkaido (pictured). She had two loves as a child: farming and drawing.

A seventeen-year-old boy named Ataru Moroboshi is chosen to play the game, and he manages to touch Lum's horns.

Urusei Yatsura developed a cult following, and in 1980 it debuted as a TV anime series in Japan. Arakawa says the quality of the artwork and story astonished her and convinced her to become a mangaka. But her family was struggling economically, and Arakawa continued to work on the farm until she was twenty-five. During this period, she continued with her painting classes and created what are called *dōjinshi* (fan manga based on popular works).

Transforming Alchemy into Manga

Few saw Arakawa's dōjinshi, but creating fan manga helped her develop her artistic style. When *Fullmetal Alchemist* was released in 2001, it was an instant hit. The story revolves around powerful officials in Amestris known as State Alchemists. While they can reshape atoms to create various items, they are forbidden from using alchemy to bring the dead back to life. After Edward and Alphonse learn alchemy, they break this taboo by resurrecting their deceased mother, Trisha.

During the attempt to re-create their mother, the Elrics violate a rigid rule of alchemy, the Law of Equivalent Exchange. The law is a founding principle of physics and chemistry. Simply stated, something cannot be created from nothing. Arakawa gave this principle her own spin, as Alphonse explained in the 2003 *Fullmetal Alchemist* anime: "Humankind cannot gain anything without first giving something in return. To obtain, something of equal value must be lost."[25]

As the Law of Equivalent Exchange relates to the story, the soul and physical body of Trisha cannot be brought back to life without an object of equal value being lost. When the Elrics try to do this, they pay a heavy price. Alphonse loses his body, becoming a giant metal cyborg. Edward loses his left leg and then his right arm when he attempts to use alchemy to restore his brother's body.

Edward's limbs are replaced by mechanical cyborg prostheses that give him superhuman fighting powers. And the metal arm and leg give Edward his name: the Fullmetal Alchemist. Edward's impressive alchemical powers are noted by the government, and he is made a State Alchemist, though he is only twelve years old. The Elrics set off on a quest to find the philosopher's stone, which has the power to restore their bodies to their original condition.

Edward is a complex character and an unlikely hero. He rarely smiles, he is cynical and snide, and his hair-trigger temper tantrums often results in catastrophe. But he is super-smart and passionate about helping the people he loves. As reviewer Jason Thompson

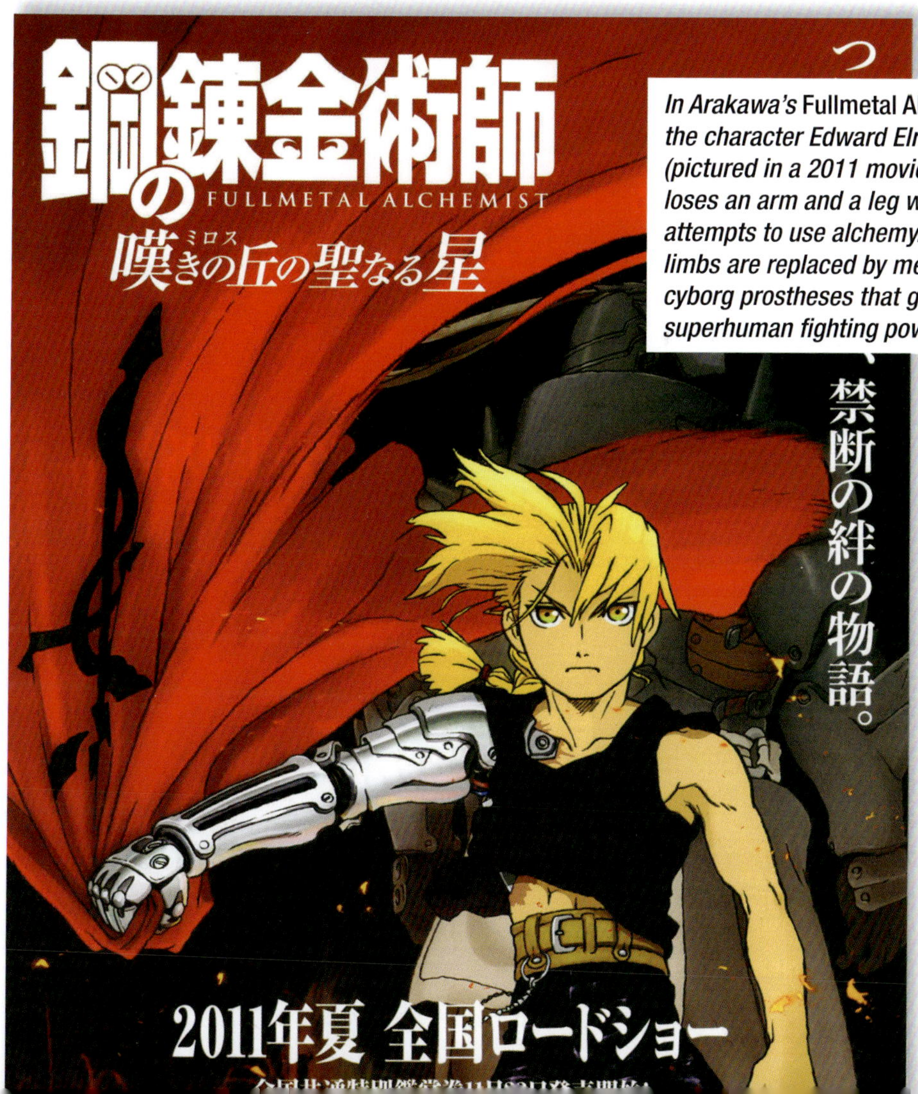

In Arakawa's Fullmetal Alchemist, *the character Edward Elric (pictured in a 2011 movie poster) loses an arm and a leg when he attempts to use alchemy. His limbs are replaced by mechanical cyborg prostheses that give him superhuman fighting powers.*

> **"Most of the *Fullmetal Alchemist* characters have two faces to their personality, a silly gag side and a deeper side; unlike some mangaka, Arakawa pulls off this delicate trick."[26]**
>
> —Jason Thompson, reviewer

writes, Arakawa has a talent for creating complicated characters: "Most of the *Fullmetal Alchemist* characters have two faces to their personality, a silly gag side and a deeper side; unlike some mangaka, Arakawa pulls off this delicate trick without destroying the believability of the series. Even the bad guys . . . are appealing while also being totally evil."[26]

While the bad guys might exhibit a humorous side, *Fullmetal Alchemist* can be very grim. The twists and turns in the plot take readers through scenes of death, destruction, war, and genocide. Arakawa enhances the gloomy mood with ample use of dark gray and black screen tone that might leave a reader squinting to see the details. But when the story veers into scenes of physical feats, violence, and frantic chases, Arakawa shows herself to be a gifted action artist. Fiends, beasts, and ogres are drawn in nightmarish detail. Fight scenes are cinematic and depicted from multiple angles. Arakawa makes good use of long-distance shots, zooming, and extreme close-ups as fighters exhibit clever moves and battle tactics. Whatever the scene, the mangaka delivers readers of shōnen manga what they want—powerful manly physiques and voluptuous women. As Arakawa explains: "If I draw them too skinny, people will think my poor characters don't eat! Men should be muscular and women should be va-va-voom!"[27]

> **"If I draw them too skinny, people will think my poor characters don't eat! Men should be muscular and women should be va-va-voom!"[27]**
>
> —Hiromu Arakawa, mangaka

While Arakawa's action scenes are dazzling, she is also known for creating intricate and accomplished female characters. She traces this skill to her childhood, growing up on a struggling dairy farm with three hardworking older sisters (and a younger brother): "Our family motto is 'those who don't work, don't deserve to eat.' Everyone has to work hard to make ends meet, including women and kids. That's the reason there are so many working women in *Fullmetal*."[28]

Working Overtime

Arakawa clearly maintains the work ethic she learned growing up on a farm. Two years after *Fullmetal Alchemist* debuted in 2001, Arakawa assisted in developing the anime series. She also worked on a second anime adaptation, the 2010 *Fullmetal Alchemist: Brotherhood*. This was happening as Arakawa was developing the final 108th chapter of the manga. According to manga journalist Caitlin Donovan, Arakawa's commitment to hard work has been amazing: "Not only did she draw and write 40-plus pages a month, she drew color illustrations, did character designs for *Fullmetal* video games, completed illustrations for

The Origins of Alchemy

When Hiromu Arakawa created *Fullmetal Alchemist* in 2001, she based the manga on the tradition of alchemy as practiced in Europe beginning in the twelfth century. During the Middle Ages alchemists used their knowledge of chemistry, biology, astronomy, and philosophy while attempting to achieve two impossible dreams. The first was transforming common metals like lead into so-called noble metals such as silver and gold. The second goal of alchemy was to discover what was called the elixir of life. This elixir would heal the sick and make humans immortal. To achieve these transformations, alchemists worked to create a magical, red powder called the philosopher's stone. This same idea appears in other literature, notably the Harry Potter stories by J.K. Rowling. Alchemists wrongly believed that the philosopher's stone could rearrange the atoms of one substance and regroup them into another substance. With the elixir of life, it was believed that the philosopher's stone could rearrange the atoms in the human body to provide health and everlasting life. All of these ideas play an important role in the complex story that is *Fullmetal Alchemist*.

light novels, and assisted in production for both anime and movies [*Fullmetal Alchemist the Movie: Conqueror of Shamballa* and *Fullmetal Alchemist: The Sacred Star of Milos*]. In order to coincide with *Brotherhood*'s release, she worked overtime and made the last chapters of *Fullmetal* 60-plus pages a month, with the last chapter over 100 pages long. In addition to all this, she had her first child in 2007 and did not take a maternity leave."[29]

Arakawa's dedication helped make *Fullmetal Alchemist* one of the most popular manga series ever created. The manga review site Dengeki Online says over 80 million volumes of the manga were sold worldwide by 2021. This gave Arakawa an estimated net worth of $64 million, according to the Idol Networth website. Arakawa is also credited with breaking down gender barriers that often prevented female mangaka from creating shōnen manga.

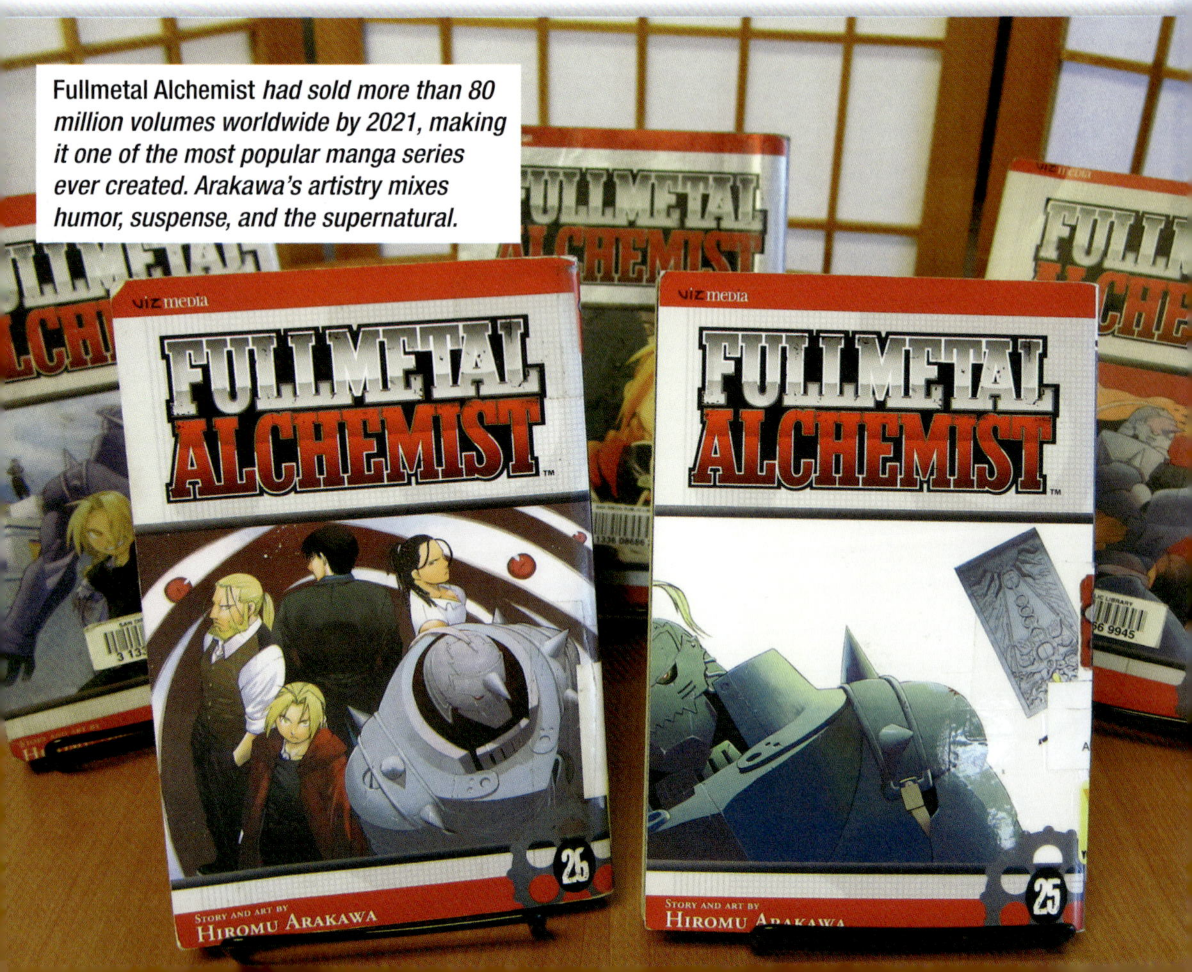

Fullmetal Alchemist ***had sold more than 80 million volumes worldwide by 2021, making it one of the most popular manga series ever created. Arakawa's artistry mixes humor, suspense, and the supernatural.***

A Woman of Action

When Hiromu Arakawa was born, her parents named her Hiromi, a name commonly given to females in Japan. When she began drawing *Fullmetal Alchemist*, Arakawa used the pen name Hiromu, which is gender neutral. Arakawa used the pen name because she was creating shōnen manga, comics for boys, and she did not want to reveal that she was a woman.

While the gender of a mangaka should not matter, women face barriers in the manga industry. There is a perception that only men can create the type of complex action stories popular in shōnen manga. In a rare interview in 2013, Arakawa challenged this commonly held belief:

> It is often said that women are better to talk about emotions, to write dialogues that hit the nail on the head, and men know how to create stories with twists and turns. As for me, I think it's difficult today to make a distinction between genres. Some men are really able to imagine sensitive and complex characters, while some women are able to create sometimes violent action scenes. Nowadays, each writer has their own specialty. It doesn't matter if they're a man or a woman.

Quoted in Clewilan, "Hiromu Arakawa Interview," Tumblr, March 9, 2013. https://clewilan.tumblr.com/post/44966298003.

After wrapping up *Fullmetal Alchemist* in 2010, Arakawa created several other critically acclaimed manga. Since 2013 she has been illustrating *The Heroic Legend of Arslan*, based on a story by Yoshiki Tanaka. The fifteenth volume of the action story about war was released in 2021, and the series sold nearly 6 million copies in the first months after its release.

Arakawa's most personal work is called *Silver Spoon*, published from 2011 to 2019. *Silver Spoon* is a coming-of-age comedy set in an agricultural high school much like the one Arakawa attended as a teenager. Arakawa created the manga to inform readers about Japan's agricultural industry while sharing information about the rewards and hardships of farming. In 2012 *Silver Spoon* was the seventh-highest-selling manga in Japan, and the award-winning series was adapted to an anime film and a live-action movie. According to Arakawa, after *Silver Spoon* was released, applications to agricultural high schools increased.

Protecting Her Privacy

Arakawa has always been very guarded about her personal life, to the point that fans cannot even find a photo of her online. But in a nod to her former life as a dairy farmer, Arakawa uses cartoon self-portraits of herself as a black-and-white Holstein cow wearing glasses. When she finally granted her first TV interview in 2017, Arakawa appeared with the cartoon cow head superimposed over her face. As she reassured viewers: "Right now, my face is cow, but I am human."[30] The rare interview was given to promote the Fullmetal Alchemist Exhibition, which displayed nine years of the manga's history at the Tokyo Dome City Gallery.

Arakawa might be publicity shy, but she does not shy away from difficult topics. *Fullmetal Alchemist* used alchemy, cyborgs, and demons to explore issues such as sexism, racial oppression, and even genocide. Arakawa might avoid the spotlight, but she lets her work speak for itself. While she might not be able to change iron into a sword, she has transformed her ink drawings into gold. And that is the kind of artistic alchemy that can only be achieved through hard work, dedication, and creative vision.

Chapter Five

Koyoharu Gotouge

Many mangaka dream of selling more than 100 million copies of a single series, but only eighteen manga artists have done so. And those who accomplished this amazing feat have usually done so over an extended period of time. For example, *Golgo 13* by Takao Saito sold 300 million tankōbon, but it has been in continuous publication since 1968. And most best-selling manga take around ten years or more to rack up huge sales. But one manga, *Demon Slayer: Kimetsu no Yaiba* by Koyoharu Gotouge, sold more than 150 million copies in a record-setting four years.

Demon Slayer, published from 2016 to 2020, is the tenth-best-selling manga of all time. (*Kimetsu no Yaiba* translates roughly as "Sword for Destruction of Demon" or "Destruction Blade for Demon.") The series follows a teenager named Tanjiro Kamado, who becomes a demon slayer to avenge the slaughter of his family by demons. While sales of the manga were about average until 2019, the release of an anime based on the series contributed to what is called a reverse influx of fans. *Demon Slayer: Kimetsu no Yaiba the Movie: Mugen Train* was so popular the tankōbon volumes of the manga sold 60 million copies in the two months after its release.

With these amazing sales figures, it is not surprising that almost everyone in Japan is familiar with *Demon Slayer*. A 2020 poll by Oricon Monitor Research found that nearly 98 percent of all Japanese people had heard of *Demon Slayer*. A separate poll by the publishing company Benesse found that Tanjiro Kamado was the number one most admired person among third- to sixth-grade schoolchildren in Japan. This gave the manga character a higher rating than the usual mothers, fathers, and teachers.

Mystery Mangaka

While Tanjiro Kamado might be a household name in Japan, the mangaka behind *Demon Slayer* is a mystery. Koyoharu Gotouge is a pen name used by the anonymous creator of the series. There are no known photos of Gotouge, who does not grant interviews.

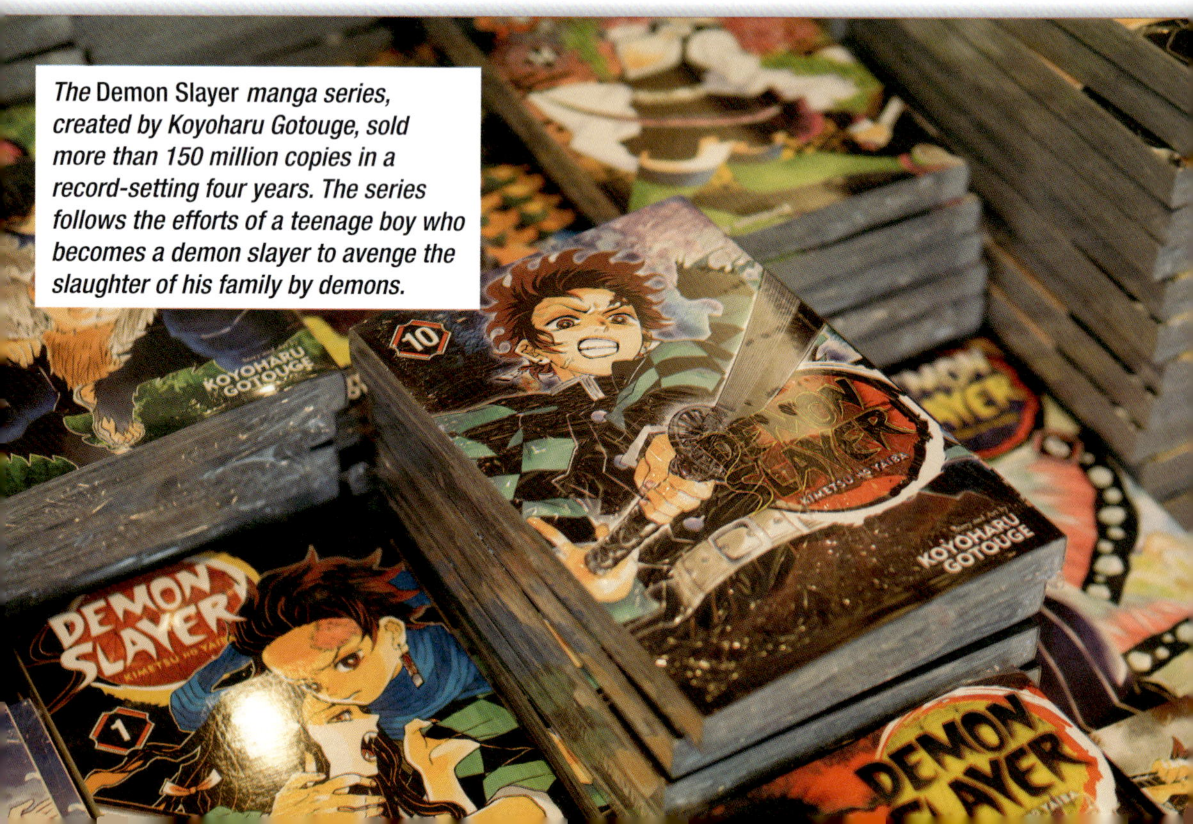

The Demon Slayer *manga series, created by Koyoharu Gotouge, sold more than 150 million copies in a record-setting four years. The series follows the efforts of a teenage boy who becomes a demon slayer to avenge the slaughter of his family by demons.*

However, there are a few facts that are known about the mangaka. The artist was born in 1989 in Fukuoka Prefecture, located on the island of Kyūshū in southern Japan. Gotouge's gender was unknown until 2020, when a worker at *Weekly Shōnen Jump* revealed that the mangaka was female. Gotouge has stated that they prefer being referred to by *they/them/their* pronouns. Their avatar, which accompanies announcements about *Demon Slayer*, is an alligator wearing glasses.

Gotouge began their manga career like many others, publishing well-received one-shots. The first work in 2013, called *Kagarigari*, was about a teenage boy who hunts a demon-like vampire. The manga won the 70th Shonen Jump Newcomer Treasure Award in 2013. Two more one-shot manga with similar themes were released in 2014. In 2015 Gotouge released *Haeniwa no Zigzag*, which featured a character named Zigzag who has the power to remove curses.

Slow Build

Gotouge hoped *Haeniwa no Zigzag* would be serialized, but the story was rejected by *Jump* as too weird and complicated for young audiences. After this failure, the mangaka conferred with their editor Tatsuhiko Katayama, who suggested creating a story based on *Kagarigari* that would be easier for readers to understand: "[*Kagarigari* has a] simple Japanese motif to it. . . . The concept of the swords and demons needed no explanation to the Japanese audience. With this we created a storyboard. . . . However, due to its serious tone, lack of comic relief and dark story, it didn't make the cut for serialization."[31] Katayama then suggested creating a lead character with a brighter personality who would provide a contrast to the dark world of demons and demon

"[*Kagarigari* has a] simple Japanese motif to it. . . . The concept of the swords and demons needed no explanation to the Japanese audience."[31]

—Tatsuhiko Katayama, manga editor

The Influence of an Editor

Koyoharu Gotouge is both successful and secretive, and the mangaka has long refused to grant interviews. But editor Tatsuhiko Katayama, who worked with Gotouge on *Demon Slayer*, was willing to explain what skills an editor needs when working with a talented mangaka like Gotouge. Katayama's comments appeared on Manga Plus, the official website of Shueisha, which publishes *Weekly Shōnen Jump* and many other popular manga:

> I feel [a manga editor] should be a motivator. It's important that they stir up the desire to keep authors going. To put it more specifically, they should be giving feedback like telling their authors what parts are interesting or how they should be doing a particular thing. There's the manager-esque parts, where they have to make the work more interesting and pick up authors when they're down. And then there's a bit of a producer's role in there, where you have to suggest to them how to sell things. Editors should be a force that draws out everything a [mangaka] has; their talent, their motivation. If they're a new talent, you also have to help them realize their full potential.

Tatsuhiko Katayama, "Demon Slayer: Kimetsu no Yaiba," Manga Plus, February 4, 2020. https://mangaplus.shueisha.co.jp.

slayers. Gotouge sketched out Tanjiro, and *Demon Slayer* was finally picked up for serialization.

Demon Slayer combines elements of dark fantasy, martial arts, and adventure. The first chapter was released in February 2016. The story is set in Japan's Taisho era, a period from 1912 to 1926 when the influence of Western technology was clashing with ancient Eastern traditions. Like countless other manga stories, *Demon Slayer* features a noble, orphaned teenager who fights evil against all odds while attempting to heal a wounded family member.

The most evil character in *Demon Slayer* is the bloodthirsty Muzan Kibutsuji. One thousand years earlier, Kibutsuji became the first person to be transformed into a demon. He is the world's most powerful demon, known as the Demon King. The minions who do his bidding are called the Twelve Demon Moons. Kibutsuji can change his appearance through cell transformation to assume the guise of various human beings, male and female, old and young. But demons, like vampires, burn to death in sunlight. The Demon King is obsessed with the idea of becoming immune to sunlight. In an attempt to develop natural immunity Kibutsuji kills most of Tanjiro's family. Tanjiro's little sister Nezuko is spared, but she is turned into a demon. While most demons are unfeeling beasts, Nezuko retains her human emotions. This prevents her from killing her brother. However, she must wear a bamboo gag over her mouth to hide her demon fangs and restrain her urge to slaughter humans.

Tanjiro takes up the blade to seek revenge against Kibutsuji. He becomes a trainee in the Demon Slayer Corps, which has worked to battle demons in secrecy for centuries. After several years of pumping up his muscles and developing his swordsmanship, Tanjiro learns several Demon Slayer superpowers. He can breathe underwater and has a heightened sense of smell that allows him to sniff out demons no matter how well they are disguised.

Gotouge created Tanjiro as a caring boy with a strong sense of justice. Unlike other Demon Slayers, Tanjiro has empathy for demons because of his sister's condition. Katayama believes Tanjiro's unique personality helped attract a legion of fans: "People don't pay for works of entertainment unless there's something different about them. . . . I think Tanjiro is a type of male main character that you don't really see much. He's so kind. He has Nezuko, so he's coming from this position where he can't just say all demons are absolute evil. He's in the gray zone."[32]

Katayama adds that Gotouge has the ability to write exceptionally interesting dialogue, which he says is a rare talent among mangaka. Gotouge claims they learned this skill reading a book on how to write novels. According to Katayama, "I'm not sure if that's really why, but there's a number of lines in the manga that resonate well. . . . They're lines you can't imagine yourself."[33]

The Eyes Tell the Story

While great lines help create an engaging story, *Demon Slayer* is drawn with flourishes that help set it apart from other manga. Gotouge inks panels with a sharp precision that gives *Demon Slayer* a clean, uncluttered look. Their most artistic drawings inspire visions of the Japanese woodblock art style known as *ukiyo-e*.

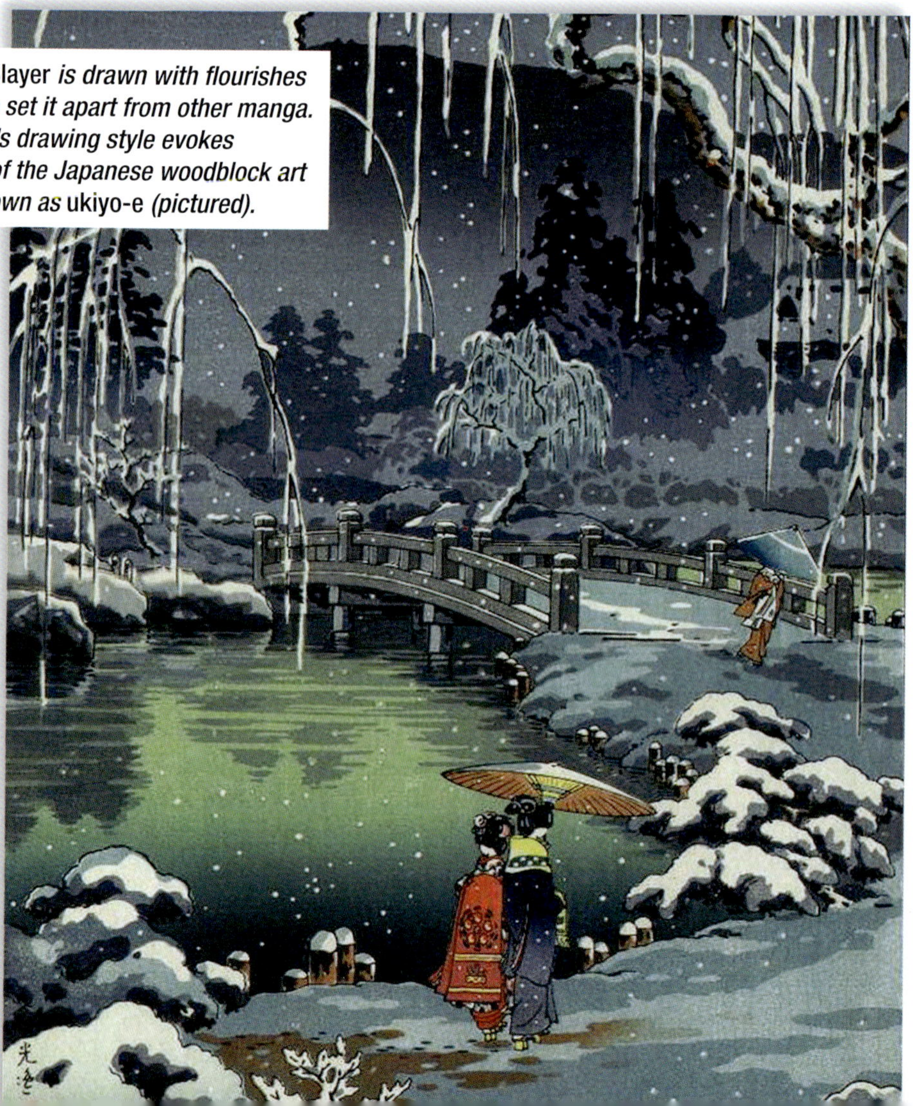

Demon Slayer *is drawn with flourishes that help set it apart from other manga. Gotouge's drawing style evokes images of the Japanese woodblock art style known as* ukiyo-e *(pictured).*

> **"Gotouge does a great job of capturing the intricate details of the muscles and inner workings of the body."[34]**
>
> —LaNeysha Campbell, manga reviewer

Other elements of *Demon Slayer* artwork reflect the modern cinematic style perfected by Osamu Tezuka. And Gotouge's extreme close-ups do more than simply add drama. Those familiar with *Demon Slayer* characters can identify individuals simply by glancing at close-up renderings of their eyes, which can be found in fan art collages circulating on social media. Gotouge illuminates the piercing gaze of the demon Muzan Kibutsuji with snake-like eyes drawn with slitted vertical pupils. Kibutsuji's Demon Moon helpers are identified by numbers tattooed on their pupils. The demon Kokushibo has three sets of eyes, while the demon Yahaba has catlike eyes on his face and a pair of green eyeballs with orange irises on his palms. The eyes of evil characters contrast with the Demon Slayers, whose large, wide eyes with dilated pupils reflect compassion.

Gotouge sometimes lets readers see through Tanjiro's eyes. Like other Demon Slayers, Tanjiro can see what is called the Transparent World. This power allows Demon Slayers to anticipate an enemy's movements by viewing their muscles, joints, and blood flow. As manga reviewer LaNeysha Campbell notes, "Gotouge does a great job of capturing the intricate details of the muscles and inner workings of the body."[34]

The eyes created by Gotouge might be considered a unique brand that works with other features to create a memorable image of each character. Like Nezuko's bamboo muzzle, these features help readers pick out characters in a crowd.

The *Demon Slayer* Anime Train

Demon Slayer's immense popularity as manga has propelled it into television and the movies. The first televised anime episode of *Demon Slayer: Kimetsu no Yaiba* premiered in Japan in April 2019. The following October it appeared on Cartoon Network's

Ukiyo-e Art and Mangaka

Some of Koyoharu Gotouge's most elaborate drawings feature elements of ukiyo-e, an art style that was popular in Japan during the seventeenth through nineteenth centuries. *Ukiyo* translates as "floating world." It refers to the culture of theaters, teahouses, and bars where Japanese people could find momentary relief from their harsh day-to-day existence. Ukiyo-e art prints, based on the Ukiyo culture, were extremely popular and could be found almost everywhere. They were created by artisans who mass-produced the prints by carving images into wooden blocks, which were coated with colored ink and pressed onto paper, like large stamps.

Ukiyo-e featured sword-wielding Samurai warriors and women known as geishas (literally "artists"), who wore white face makeup, pretty silk kimonos, and flowers in their elaborately styled hair. Rather than focus on realism, ukiyo-e artists, much like Gotouge, worked to capture feelings ranging from humor to fright. According to manga journalists Sheri Le and Will Dodds, "Available as scrolls, greeting cards, book illustrations or single prints, ukiyo-e depicted caricatures of people, landscapes, the uncertainty of life and sensual pleasures . . . in a familiar Japanese style. . . . Akin to the manga of today, ukiyo-e was . . . cheap to produce, widely circulated, and consistent with the spirit of play or entertainment."

Sheri Le and Will Dodds, "Manga: Evolution," Right Stuf, 2021. www.rightstufanime.com.

Adult Swim nighttime programming in the United States. The twenty-six episodes covered the first seven volumes of Gotouge's original manga. The TV series generated universal acclaim as reviewers praised the show for its animation quality, digital effects, and lovable protagonists Tanjiro and Nezuko. The series received numerous honors, including Anime of the Year at the 2020 Crunchyroll Anime Awards. A second season of the TV anime, called *Kimetsu no Yaiba: Yūkaku Hen*, premiered in 2021.

The full-length anime *Demon Slayer: Kimetsu no Yaiba the Movie: Mugen Train* premiered in October 2020. *Mugen Train* was based on an original story by Gotouge and picks up where the first season of the TV series left off. Tanjiro, Nezuko, and the others take on a new mission—investigating the mysterious disappearance of forty people from a train. The weekend the anime debuted in Japan, it made a record-setting $313 million. This made *Mugen Train* the highest-grossing movie opening in Japanese history and the second-highest-grossing anime of all time. As journalist Kat Moon writes, "[This was] a surreal achievement that only deepened interest in the mysterious author and illustrator at the franchise's heart."[35]

The mystery continued to deepen in 2021 when Gotouge was honored by *Time* magazine in the TIME100 Next List. This annual edition features one hundred up-and-coming artists, musicians, leaders, and innovators who are making history and whose influence is expected to remain relevant in the future. The *Time* article noted that little is known about the person who goes by the name Gotouge. But one of the editors who works with the mangaka, Kohei Onishi, told *Time* that the artist's personality is reflected in Tanjiro's "serious nature, honesty and strong sense of responsibility."[36]

"[*Mugen Train*'s success is] a surreal achievement that only deepened interest in the mysterious author and illustrator at the franchise's heart."[35]

—Kat Moon, journalist

While the public might never learn more about the enigmatic creator of *Demon Slayer*, their work stands for itself. And maybe more will be revealed about the mangaka in their next series, which Gotouge promises to be a science fiction romantic comedy. Whatever is next from the mysterious mangaka, fans can be sure that the story will be complex and the artwork intriguing. As Katayama notes, Gotouge "just keeps drawing and drawing, so much so that it's hard to keep up."[37]

Source Notes

Introduction: Mangaka Make Art

1. Quoted in Cynthia Medina, "Rutgers Professor Explores Varying Themes in Japanese and American Comics," Rutgers Today, December 5, 2019. www.rutgers.edu.
2. Quoted in Goodreads, "Osamu Tezuka: Quotes," 2021. www.goodreads.com.

Chapter One: Osamu Tezuka

3. Quoted in Van Gogh Alive, "Artists in 60 Seconds: Tezuka Osamu," 2021. www.vangoghgenova.it.
4. Quoted in Helen McCarthy, *The Art of Osamu Tezuka*. New York: Abrams ComicArts, 2009, p. 81.
5. Frederik L. Schodt, *The Astro Boy Essays*. Berkeley, CA: Stone Bridge, 2007, p. 30.
6. Quoted in Schodt, *The Astro Boy Essays*, p. 21.
7. Kris Kosaka, "'Phoenix': Osamu Tezuka's Epoch-Spanning Manga Masterpiece," *Japan Times*, June 11, 2016. www.japantimes.co.jp.
8. Quoted in Van Gogh Alive, "Artists in 60 Seconds."

Chapter Two: Naoko Takeuchi

9. Paul Gravett, *Manga: Sixty Years of Japanese Comics*. New York: Harper Design International, 2004, p. 79.
10. Quoted in Sailor Moon, "1996 Naoko Takeuchi Interview in Animerica Magazine," September 25, 2018. www.sailormoonforum.com.
11. Quoted in Sailor Moon, "1996 Naoko Takeuchi Interview in Animerica Magazine."
12. Quoted in Miss Dream, "Naoko Takeuchi Interview ROLa Magazine September 2013," 2021. https://missdream.org.

13. Quoted in Sailor Moon, "1996 Naoko Takeuchi Interview in Animerica Magazine."
14. Quoted in Miss Dream, "Naoko Takeuchi Interview ROLa Magazine January 2014," 2021. https://missdream.org.
15. Jessica Lord, "Sailor Moon: Positive Female Role Model Since 1992," Tofugu, May 5, 2014. www.tofugu.com.

Chapter Three: Eiichiro Oda

16. Quoted in Misaki C. Kido, "Interview: Eiichiro Oda," Viz, April 2, 2012. www.viz.com.
17. Quoted in the Grandline, "Tell Me Oda Sensei," 2020. www.thegrandline.com.
18. Quoted in *The One Piece Podcast*, "One Piece to Celebrate 20th Anniversary in Weekly Shonen Jump," November 29, 2016. www.onepiecepodcast.com.
19. Juan de Dios Dougnac, "One Piece-Manga Series Review," Fantasy-Faction, April 24, 2013. http://fantasy-faction.com.
20. Quoted in Kido, "Interview."
21. Quoted in Zach Logan, "'One Piece' Is Actually 70% Through the Story, Probably," *The One Piece Podcast*, July 23, 2016. www.onepiecepodcast.com.
22. Quoted in Zach Logan, "Eiichiro Oda Addresses Health Concerns, Sleep Schedule in 'One Piece' Newspaper," *The One Piece Podcast*, July 20, 2016. www.onepiecepodcast.com.
23. Quoted in Joseph Luster, "One Piece 1000th Chapter Celebration Has the Series Going All Out," Otaku USA Magazine, January 3, 2021. https://otakuusamagazine.com.

Chapter Four: Hiromu Arakawa

24. Quoted in Clewilan, "Hiromu Arakawa Interview," Tumblr, March 9, 2013. https://clewilan.tumblr.com/post/44966298003.
25. Quoted in Phil Archbold, "The Untold Truth of Fullmetal Alchemist," Looper, December 12, 2019. www.looper.com.
26. Jason Thompson, "Jason Thompson's House of 1000 Manga—Fullmetal Alchemist," Anime News Network, June 6, 2013. www.animenewsnetwork.com.
27. Quoted in Caitlin Donovan, "Get to Know a Manga Artist: The Unstoppable Hiromu Arakawa," Mary Sue, October 14, 2014. www.themarysue.com.
28. Quoted in Donovan, "Get to Know a Manga Artist."

29. Donovan, "Get to Know a Manga Artist."
30. Quoted in Archbold, "The Untold Truth of Fullmetal Alchemist."

Chapter Five: Koyoharu Gotouge

31. Tatsuhiko Katayama, "Demon Slayer: Kimetsu no Yaiba," Manga Plus, February 4, 2020. https://mangaplus.shueisha.co.jp.
32. Katayama, "Demon Slayer."
33. Katayama, "Demon Slayer."
34. LaNeysha Campbell, "Advanced Review: 'Demon Slayer: Kimetsu no Yaiba,' Volume 18," *But Why Tho?*, October 24, 2020. https://butwhythopodcast.com.
35. Kat Moon, "Koyoharu Gotouge," *Time*, February 17, 2021. https://time.com.
36. Quoted in Moon, "Koyoharu Gotouge."
37. Katayama, "Demon Slayer."

For Further Research

Books

Robert M. Henderson, *A Quick Guide to Anime and Manga*. San Diego, CA: ReferencePoint, 2022.

Helen McCarthy, *The Art of Osamu Tezuka*. New York: Abrams ComicArts, 2009.

Frederik L. Schodt, *Manga! Manga! The World of Japanese Comics*. Tokyo: Kodansha, 2013.

Dalia Sharawna, *Manga Art Secrets*. New York: Search Press, 2021.

Gianni Simone, *Otaku Japan: The Fascinating World of Japanese Manga, Anime, Gaming, Cosplay, Toys, Idols and More!* North Clarendon, VT: Tuttle, 2021.

Akira Toriyama, *Dragon Ball: A Visual History*. San Francisco, CA: VIZ Media, 2019.

Internet Sources

Phil Archbold, "The Untold Truth of Fullmetal Alchemist," Looper, December 12, 2019. www.looper.com.

Clewilan, "Hiromu Arakawa Interview," Tumblr, March 9, 2013. https://clewilan.tumblr.com/post/44966298003.

Caitlin Donovan, "Get to Know a Manga Artist: The Unstoppable Hiromu Arakawa," Mary Sue, October 14, 2014. www.themarysue.com.

Tatsuhiko Katayama, "Demon Slayer: Kimetsu no Yaiba," Manga Plus, February 4, 2020. https://mangaplus.shueisha.co.jp.

Misaki C. Kido, "Interview: Eiichiro Oda," Viz, April 2, 2012. www.viz.com.

Jessica Lord, "Sailor Moon: Positive Female Role Model Since 1992," Tofugu, May 5, 2014. www.tofugu.com.

Joseph Luster, "One Piece 1000th Chapter Celebration Has the Series Going All Out," Otaku USA Magazine, January 3, 2021. https://otakuusamagazine.com.

Sailor Moon, "1996 Naoko Takeuchi Interview in Animerica Magazine," September 25, 2018. www.sailormoonforum.com.

Websites

Anime News Network
www.animenewsnetwork.com

A comprehensive site covering anime and manga with news, views of latest releases, discussion forums, and an encyclopedia of terms and titles.

Comics Worth Reading
http://comicsworthreading.com

The website offers independent opinion about manga and comic books along with news, reviews, author biographies, and podcasts.

Demon Slayer: Kimetsu No Yaiba
www.viz.com/demon-slayer-kimetsu-no-yaiba

The official website for the *Demon Slayer* manga features preview copies, past volumes of the series, and anime trailers.

One Piece
https://one-piece.com

The English-language version of the *One Piece* website features details about the more than one-thousand-chapter manga drawn by Eiichiro Oda. Readers can learn about the story and the characters, watch anime clips, and shop for related merchandise.

Tokyo Otaku Mode
https://otakumode.com

Otaku describes a young Japanese person obsessed with manga and anime. This site covers the latest pop culture news from Japan, with a focus on manga, anime, games, music, and fashion.

Index